Bravo Yadav

Journey of Honorary Captain Subedar Yogendra Singh Yadav
India's Youngest Param Vir Chakra Recipient

Bravo Yadav

Journey of Honorary Captain Subedar Yogendra Singh Yadav
India's Youngest Param Vir Chakra Recipient

Dr. Deepak Singh

HAR-ANAND
PUBLICATIONS PVT LTD

Special Thanks to
Chitrangda Singh
CS Films LLP

HAR-ANAND PUBLICATIONS PVT LTD
E-49/3, Okhla Industrial Area, Phase-II, New Delhi-110020
Tel.: 41603490
E-mail: info@haranandbooks.com/haranand@rediffmail.com
Shop online at: www.haranandbooks.com
@haranand_publications
Har Anand Publications

Reprint, 2024

Published by Ashok Gosain and Ashish Gosain for
Har-Anand Publications Pvt Ltd

Printed in India at Vinayak Offset

To

The soldiers who laid their lives for the nation

Foreword

Har-Anand Publications has decided to launch a new series of translation of Punjabi literature. It is a welcome initiative to take Punjabi authors beyond the borders of Punjab through translation into English. There is no hesitation in accepting that despite having created a rich body of work, Punjabi literature is not being widely read. A large section of Punjabi population, who have got education in English medium schools, feel at home more with English than Punjabi. They prefer English to be their language of self-expression. It is also globally accepted that one can open his or her soul in one's mother tongue only. While such educated people express their urban experiences in English, Punjabi language and culture are at a disadvantage. Consequently, the purity of Punjabi culture, the essence of its land, the lifestyle of the people, its traditions, heroic tales and stories are missing in their sensibilities.

For those who can't read Punjabi, translation acts like a bridge. It is a commendable initiative taken by the publisher to promote Punjabi literature through translation. It is also important to realize the specific significance of translating Punjabi literature into English that has a wider readership. A large number of overseas Punjabi readers would get a chance to appreciate the richness of Punjabi literature and then go on to bring more texts to their respective countries, which may in turn make the Har-Anand to publish more books of vernacular languages for them.

Punjabi literature has a glorious history. It started with the hymns of the Sufi saint, Sheikh Farid. It was further enriched by other Sufi poets such as Shah Hussain, Sultan Bahu, Bulleh Shah and many others. Bhakti movement contributed a lot to enrich Punjabi literature. Though Guru Granth Sahib is a religious text of Sikh Religion, it is considered to be one of the best literature ever created on this land. The Tenth Sikh Master, Guru Gobind Singh, who himself was a great poet, had 52 poets in his court. Authors of love legends of Punjab like Heer Ranjha, Sohni Mahiwal, Mirza Sahiban, Sassi Punnu etc. also played a significant role in the development of Punjabi literature. Similarly, the bards of Punjab also played their role in enriching it. Thus, the secular content of our literature transcends the religious divide and communal sentiments, which at times is fueled by the vested groups. After the accession of the Punjab in 1849, the Victorian novel, Elizabethan drama, free verse and modernism entered into Punjabi literature through the introduction of English education system during the British rule. This brought new genres as well as movements to Punjabi literature.

Now we are embarking on a new terrain by introducing new literary works authored by the Punjabi writers in English, thus, trying to widen the spectrum of our series of Punjabi books into English. According to us Punjabi populace living in any part of the world share similar sensibilities and literature created by them in any of the language is presentation of same sensibility, so it comes under the ambit of Punjabi literature. Idea behind publication of these books of Punjabi authors is to bring fore front the creativity of our authors who are living in different parts of the globe.

The book under publication *'The Bravo Yadav'* is a biography of Subedar Major and Honorary Captain Yogendra Singh Yadav by Dr. Deepak Singh. Yogendra Singh Yadav is remembered for his bravery in Kargil war where he enlisted with the 18 Grenadiers. He was part of the Ghatak Platoon and was assigned to capture Tiger Hill during Kargil War. The Platoon had to climb more than sixteen hundred feet of a steep snowbound and rocky section of the mountain to reach on the peak of Tiger Hill. He volunteered to lead and fix the rope for his team. On seeing the team, the enemy opened extreme automatic grenade, rocket and artillery fire. The Commander and two of his colleagues died in firing and the Platoon was installed. He then crawled up to the enemy position in tranquility, and in process, he sustained multiple injuries. He continued climbing in the forward direction towards the enemy's direction, lobbed grenades, continued firing from his weapons and executed many of the enemy soldiers in close combat. Inspired by his valorous act, the Platoon charged on the other positions and captured Tiger Hill Top. He survived 12 bullets on his body, with one bullet piercing through his heart. The Param Vir Chakra was announced for him posthumously, but soon it was found that he was recovering in a hospital and there was another soldier with his namesake in the company who was martyred during Kargil war. Thus his biography is a great source of inspiration for all of us. Dr. Deepak Singh has weaved his life history in a way that one can't resist to complete reading without any break.

I express thanks from core of my heart to Shri Narendra Kumar, Chairman, Har-Anand Publications, a pioneer in publishing industry, for choosing me and giving me responsibility to act as the Editor of this new series. My heartiest gratitude to Dr. Deepak Singh, author of the book, for showing belief in me and our publishing house and for giving rights to publish this book. Hope readers will welcome this venture.

Prof. Rawail Singh
Former Head, Department of Punjabi,
University of Delhi

Preface

Yogendra Singh Yadav, a young ordinary boy from a small village in Aurangabad Ahir weaves an extraordinary tale through his journey as a soldier in the Indian Army fighting in the Kargil War, 1999. Like any other young village boy, Yogendra had a childhood filled with frolic. However, the determination in him to serve his country made him different the others. Yogendra's courage and will not only drives him through the experience of the Kargil War but also lands him as the sole survivor to be honoured with the most prestigious Param Vir Chakra.

Dr. Deepak Singh

Contents

I

Childhood

The soft sensation of the soil and the kiss of the wind on the face were the earliest of Yogendra Singh's memories. Born in a small village named Aurangabad Ahir in the Bulandshahr district of Uttar Pradesh, Yogendra Singh Yadav was a boy born with a large vision. Yogendra's family consisted of his parents and two brothers, one younger and the other elder to him. On a bright sunny summer morning, Yogendra's father Karan Singh Yadav had returned home to the news of his new born son. Karan Singh, a soldier in the Indian Army, had to be away from his family most of the time. During the birth of his youngest son Yogendra, he was posted on duty. On a seemingly uneventful day, Karan Singh was called to the administrative office. The clerk had knocked at their dorm, "Singh, there is an urgent call from your home." Karan had been waiting for this call, since he came back with the knowledge of his wife Santara being pregnant. He ran in a single breathe to get the call waiting for him. The official directed him towards the receiver and Karan picked it up, "Hello?" Karan's nephew recognized his voice and quickly answered, "Uncle, you must return soon. Aunt is in labour." That is all he needed to hear. Karan quickly packed his things and took permission to leave on an urgent basis.

Cellular phones were not common during those days, therefore, Karan Singh had no way of knowing the news back at home. All through his long journey, his mind remained lost. His eyes remained fixated on the passing view from the window seat of the bus. The fellow passenger looked at the bobbing feet of Karan. Looking at the tensed soldier, the old man spoke, "Son, is everything alright?"

Karan's trance was broken, "Everything is fine, Sir. Why do you ask?" The old man smiled, "Your leg tells me otherwise." Karan gave out a loud laugh at the old man's sharp observation, "My wife is giving birth to our child, Sir. They are probably in the world by now. I am hurrying back home to my family." The old man held out his hand and touched his head, "Bless you, son. You will have a healthy and beautiful baby." Karan felt a lot more assured and at ease after the conversation. Some people, he felt, had a calming effect on others and it did truly help him.

Karan Singh returned to a crowd of people gathered around his home. Neighbours and relatives had come to welcome the new soul. When the group saw Karan they moved aside to let him in. Some even stopped to talk to him. Karan was desperate to go inside his wife's room. He saw his nephew at the entrance. The young man came rushing towards him, "Uncle, you have a healthy baby boy." Karan was relieved to hear about the baby, "What about your aunt?" The young man assured, "She is doing we'll. You must go inside now." Karan was now completely comfortable and existed to meet the new member. When he entered the room, he noticed his eldest son, Jitendra sitting quietly in a chair by his mother's bed. This child had always been the best-behaved in the lot. Karan watched his wife stir which meant she was half awake. As soon as he approached the bed and she noticed him, she completely woke up with a huge smile. There was a twinkle in her eyes, watching her man return to their baby. They both had a reserved relationship where none of them were overly expressive. Silently gestures and fleeting glances were their agents of communication and affection.

Karan touched Santara's hand, "Are you okay?" Sanata nodded her and pointed towards the cradle. Karan moved slowly to not wake up the children. As he looked inside the cradle, a pair of black beady eyes stared back at him. The child was so quite that one wouldn't have known that he was awake. Karan picked up the baby in his arms and his heart filled with warmth. The sweet fragrance of the new born spread in his senses. He swayed in a slow-dance like motion. The baby gave out a soft smile seeming to enjoy it. There was no loud crying or screaming the entire time. Karan was amazed by the boy's calm aura. Strangely, Karan had a feeling of wonder watching this infant as if he was born to do great things. He smiled at his foolish thoughts thinking it's only a father's wishful for their children. Karan spoke softly, "My commando, Yogendra, you are going to make daddy so proud, aren't you?" Karan himself did not know how true his words would ring in the future.

A carefree infancy accompanied Yogendra in the early years of his life which lasted for a little while. Yogendra spent his initial days running around the field, climbing trees, and playing with his friends. Despite his notorious nature, Yogendra was loved by all for his innocence. The peaceful village life was quite a contrast to the robust energy of the young mischievous boys. These recollections had often provided him strength in later life. The simplicity of his belonging had added to Yogendra's character. Although he had begun to dream big from a tender age, Yogendra's perspective towards life was a reflection of his humble and simple nature.

Yogendra was quite well-known for his mischiefs in school and the village. They were a band of boys always planning some notorious strategy. Yogendra was their unsaid leader taking charge of situations. They were often caught climbing trees and picking mangoes from Harinath's garden. One of the days after school, Yogendra had convinced the boys with his plan to pick mangoes. The memory of the sour unripe mangoes were enough reason for the boys to not need much convincing. To set an example, Yogendra entered the garden first and quickly climbed the tree. Then he began throwing the mangoes at his friend. In the meantime, Harinath had spotted them. He released his dogs to chase the boys out of his premises. The ones outside the fence started screaming for Yogendra to escape from the beasts. Yogendra jumped from the tall tree in a go. Yogendra on the run was so fast that all attempts to catch him failed. Harinath's complaints at home would lead to occasional punishment but that did not discourage the boys. Even in school, they were often seen outside the classroom enduring some punishment of the other. Playing pranks on classmates was the reason of raucous in the classroom. Although the boys indulged in mischievous activities, they did their studies properly which was the reason they were mostly spared by the teachers and parents.

Although Yogendra enjoyed the freedom, his household also maintained discipline. His father being an ex-army official had raised the boys with responsibility. From an early childhood, Yogendra's father had inculcated the patriotic feelings within his children. His father's views about serving the nation had created a room within Yogendra. He and his brother would often sit beside their father listening to stories about soldiers and the army. Yogendra's father's experience in the army got his children also interested in the life of a soldier. Yogendra would run around the fields holding the national flag in his hands and screaming "Bharat Mata Ki Jaay" at the top of his voice which he had learnt from his father. Whenever Yogendra's father came back home, he would take the children to the carnival in the village. Yogendra would always insist his father to buy him the toy gun. When asked about his purpose of buying the gun, he would proudly declare, "I will defeat all enemies with this gun." His father would enjoy a good laugh watching the little child's enthusiasm. No one had then anticipated that the seed of the patriotic passion would later grow into a huge tree.

Yogendra and his friends were also friendly and helpful, so people always remembered them. When Yogendra was 10 years old, he would go swimming with his friends in a huge pond, at a little distance from his house. In summer, this was the most refreshing activity enjoyed by the boys. They would take plunges in the pond and perform different tricks. One day, Gopal, Yogendra's friend, had dived into the pool from a distance. The boys were all involved in swimming and relaxing by themselves. After some time Yogendra noticed that Gopal was missing. Without a second though, the small boy swam deep to find his friend. Yogendra was the best swimmer of the lot, yet for his age it was difficult to manoeuvre at the deep end of the pond. He located Gopal's form floating and quickly pulled him along. Somehow the other boys came and together they pulled Gopal out. He had hit his head on a rock and fainted instantly. The villagers came running from nearby and took the boy to the clinic. Gopal quickly recovered consciousness and his family was thankful to Yogendra. Although the boys received scolding from their families but Yogendra was also praised for his bravery.

Yogendra was still a teenager who went about creating mischief. This was the growing age and inquisition was at it's peak and so was peer influence. On a summer evening, during holidays, Yogendra was lying in a room on the roof with his brother. As soon as his brother left, Yogendra lit a smoke that he had saved in his stack. Yogendra, like most other boys in his class, had picked up the habit of smoking tobacco-filled leaves. He and his friends had developed a taste for it and often stole it from elders. Yogendra saved the money that he sometimes received from his brother to buy 'beedies'. He looked under the mattress and easily found the packet. This was his hideout. Yogendra's brother had gone downstairs to sleep. This was the safest time to consume it. Yogendra was still scared of his brother catching him. So, he had to be cautious all the time. Only when his brother was not in the vicinity did he attempt to indulge himself.

Yogendra lit the smoke with a matchstick that he had taken from the prayer room. He peacefully took a drag and relished it, laying back on the bed. He was on his second drag when his brother arrived out of nowhere. Yogendra's luck was not on his side. His brother had forgotten his jar, so he came back to fetch it. Yogendra heard the sound of the footsteps and quickly threw away the object and attempted to make himself presentable. He managed to hide the object but he could not manage the smell. Jitendra entered the room and looked straight at Yogendra. His face indicated that he detected something out of place. Jitendra moved closer to Yogendra and started smelling his clothes, "Were you smoking?" Yogendra confidently lied or so he thought, "No, I don't smoke." Jitendra pinned him with his stare, "Are you sure? Open your mouth." Yogendra slightly parted his mouth. Jitendra enquired, "Do you have problems with your mouth? Should I do it myself?" Yogendra did not want to piss his brother off more than he was going to be. He opened his mouth wide and a strong smell of tobacco hit Jitendra, "You are lying. Get up!" Yogendra got up and away from the bed. Jitendra began searching for his stash. He did not have to put in much effort. A packet 'bidi' was found under the bed.

Jitendra did not say another word and started beating Yogendra. His hands randomly hit against all parts of his body. When Jitendra noticed no hint of regret in Yogendra's body language, he crushed his pack of smoke. Yogendra still did not repent. He was extremely angry, "Why did you do that? I won,'t eat tonight." Jitendra gave out a mocking laughter, "And you think you can survive without food? How long will you go on without it?" Yogendra replied sternly, "Until you all bring me a pack of smoke, I will not eat." Jitendra screamed, "Then you won't eat. Live with it." Jitendra angrily stormed out of the room and informed his parents, "This boy is getting out of our hands. Today he is smoking. Tomorrow, who knows what he is going to do. He demands for a smoke which is his condition to eat food. Let him be. No one is going to give him any food. I wonder how long he can sustain." What Jitendra did not know was that this was going to be a long haul.

Yogendra did not eat for seven days. Yogendra's mother tried to convince him everyday, "Don't be so stubborn. Eat your food." Yogendra remained resolute, "Give me smoke. I will eat the food." His mother shook her head, "What is happening with you? I will not give you anything of that sort. If your father returns and watches you still continuing with your charade, he is going to be very angry." Yogendra did not reply. At that point, he cared about nothing but his ego which had been hurt by his brother. He was not mature enough to understand the implications of his action. All he knew was that he had to have a smoke. Yogendra's father returned home to the ongoing drama from her sister's house in a few days. Yogendra was called inside his father's room. All the members of his family had gathered there. Yogendra's father had been reading a newspaper while sitting in his chair. His father looked up from his paper, "I heard you are still not eating. How long are you going to disobey us? Yogendra remained silent. His father screamed, "Answer my question. What is it that you want?" Yogendra looked into his eyes, "I want a smoke." He was an extremely stubborn boy and definitely fearless. Yogendra's father lost his cool, "That is it. I have had enough of your nonsense. Jitendra beats him till he eats the food."

Jitendra hit Yogendra with whatever he could find in his hand. Yogendra's skin turned black and blue but he did not make any sound. Eventually, Jitendra got tired but Yogendra remained in place. When the beating stopped, Yogendra lost his patience, "I don't want to stay here anymore. I am out of here." Without any more justifications, he ran. His brother began running after him with his cousins. His parents followed behind them. When they saw Yogendra running towards the Ganga canal, they got scared. They assumed that Yogendra was going to jump inside the canal. However, Yogendra was not a fool. He was definitely not going to give his life over a pack of smokes. Yogendra simply wanted to escape from his family. When the villagers saw them running, they became worried, "What happened?" Yogendra's mother panted, "Yogendra is going to jump in the canal." The villagers were shocked. They dropped all their work and ran after them. His brother screamed towards the farmers who were cutting the wheat, "Someone catch the boy. He is running towards the canal." More villagers joined the chase.

After about eight kilometers of running, Yogendra felt an intense pain in his stomach. His body had been deprived of food for a long time and could not manage the strenuous activity. Yogendra dropped to the ground. The villagers and his family members got hold of him. They used thick rods to beat him and bring him back home. Yogendra still refused to eat as his demand had not been fulfilled. One of Yogendra's father's friend came home to talk to him. When Yogendra's father told his friend about Yogendra's action, he asked to take him home. Yogendra agreed to go along with him. When Yogendra reached his father's friend's house, they offered him a lot of food. Yogendra stated, "There is food at my home. I don't want it." The man enquired, "Then what do you want? Why are you not eating?" Yogendra promptly replied, "I will only eat once I get a smoke." The man knew there was no other way to win over the boy, "I will give you a smoke now only if you promise not to make it a habit."

Yogendra nodded and took the offered cigarette. The man insisted that he eats but he wanted to go home and have his meal. Yogendra knew no one was going to offer him any food now but the vow had been completed and he could eat. So, he decided to do all the work in the field to win over his family. When his parents noticed that he was making an effort, they decided to offer him food. This stubbornness in his nature which had been a disadvantage in this event did eventually help him in his future actions.

The innocence of childhood was short-lived for Yogendra. When Yogendra was in the fifth standard, his father got bedridden due to asthma and other illnesses. The technological advancement in the village was slow, therefore, availing proper treatment was difficult. One of Yogendra's cousin sisters, who lived in Faridabad, had taken his father to the city. It was easier to get treated and reach the hospital in times of emergency in the city. With the exit of Yogendra's father from their home, life for them had turned miserable. The three young boys with their mother were left in a troublesome phase with the only source of income being cut-off. Yogendra's elder brother, Jitendra took charge of the situation. Jitendra was only a child studying in the seventh standard at that time but overnight the crisis had made him a man. He received help from the neighbours to learn to farm. People gave directions but all work had to be done by Jitendra. Farming was the only possible solution for the family to survive. They already had all tools at home, to begin with the task. They had a bull that assisted Jitendra to plough the fields and plant the seeds. Gradually, he learnt all the techniques and executed the process of farming with accuracy.

Yogendra, on the other hand, was still an adolescent who did not realize the intensity of the situation at home. He still desired to enjoy his youthful days with his friends. Yogendra did not have any interest in farming and he did not understand his duty in that situation. Yogendra's mother would always accompany his brother to the field and help him with farming. They had livestock at home and there were numerous duties associated with them. Usually, most responsibilities would be managed by Jitendra and their mother. On one of the days, there was more work on the field. Yogendra's mother had gone to the field with his brother. Yogendra was instructed to complete all chores at home and take care of the animals. Yogendra was easily distracted by his friend who had come with the proposition to play kabaddi. Yogendra's childish heart could not resist and he followed his friend to the playground. They played until the sky had turned dark. Yogendra had completely forgotten about his chores while he was enjoying himself with his friends. However, as the time arrived to return home, Yogendra felt his heart dip down to his stomach. There was an aura of nervous energy around him and his gut did not feel quite positively supported.

Yogendra tip-toed into his house, hoping no one would notice his arrival. The stars were not in his favour. His mother was doing her work on the patio. Soon, Yogendra's brother walked out of his room. The expression on his brother's face froze Yogendra on the spot. He realized that his brother was already aware that all chores were left unattended at home and his arrival at this hour clearly hinted where he had been. Without uttering a single word, Jitendra moved towards his brother. Before Yogendra could have comprehended, a sharp sting on his cheek and a loud ringing in his ears announced the slap. Jitendra's voice loomed loud, "This is my first and last attempt to make you understand the gravity of our situation. Our father is not at home, therefore all the responsibilities are now ours. If we shy away from our duties and behave callously, the entire village is going to laugh at us. They will mock us for being useless sons and not taking care of our mother and household when our father is sick. If we fulfill our responsibilities wholeheartedly, the same people will praise us for successfully managing the crisis. So what do you want? Praises or criticism?"

Jitendra's words planted roots in Yogendra's heart. He had a sudden realization of his mistakes and wanted to correct himself. When Yogendra watched his young brother sacrifice his childhood for his duties towards the family, he decides to help him in every possible way. The hard labour of farming was still being managed by Jitendra. However, Jitendra took up the responsibility of the household chores. Yogendra imitated his brother and started to learn from his actions on the farm. The brothers were still very young to manage all the problems at home. They were not proficient at ploughing and farming. Often equipment broke or tools were needed and the brothers had to rely on the neighbours. Work got disrupted when things did not go as planned. Sometimes they had to travel to Meerut to get equipment repaired. As they were amateur and ignorant, people had often duped them by charging more for services. They were not prepared for the cunning world where people wait for the opportunity to grab and steal. Every day was a struggle for the boys who were learning the ropes to survive in the world without much assistance from people.

There was one person who had been a guardian to the brothers in the absence of their father which is their cousin brother. Yogendra's elder uncle and aunt had passed away long before he was born. The orphaned children of his uncle had found their family with them. The two daughters and one son of Yogendra's uncle had been brought up by his mother like her own. Yogendra's cousin brother was much elder to him, therefore treated him like a child. The entire family respected his opinions and orders. Although he never raised hands at the children everyone feared his authority. He was a huge man with a steel gaze that could hardly be endured by a kid. Yogendra's household did not have a television. To watch programs, all the kids and adults in the village went to his relative's house who was the only one to own a television. Yogendra would be impatiently waiting for Fridays and Saturdays as he knew there would be movies being played on these specific days on some channels. As the night would rolled in, all children made their beds with pillows and sneaked out through the windows to watch movies. Yogendra would climb the rear wall of his house to go to his aunt's house as soon as clock stroke eleven for the movie to begin. Hardly would he have enjoyed thirty minutes of his freedom, when his cousin brother would come looking for him. Yogendra's cousin brother would silently walk up behind him, "Did you think you could deceive me?" Yogendra's throat would go dry at the moment and pulse would rise. He did not dare challenge his brother's instructions. There was also immense respect in Yogendra's heart for his cousins. His brother's instincts of supervision were so strong that he always knew what the children were up to. His guidance had a positive effect on Yogendra and added discipline to this character.

Yogendra's father, Karan Singh Yadav had been an ex-Indian army officer who had been part of the Kumaon regiment. Yogendra's father had wanted his brother to apply for the Indian army when Jitendra was in the tenth standard. Jitendra wanted to continue his studies at that point and thought he was too young to apply. He waited a few years and completed his preliminary studies. Jitendra started making attempts for the army since 1994 but success was not immediate. When Jitendra was in the second year of his B.S.E course, he got selected in the Indian army for the EME division in 1995. Jitendra was elated to finally join the army and walk in his father's footsteps to serve the nation. His mother, however, was heartbroken just as any mother would feel. She could not absorb the pain of separation from her child. Jitendra was the eldest son and his departure would change a lot of things at home which was difficult for his mother. The family relied on Jitendra for managing the household chores and farming. Their mother was worried that this will start moving downhill once her eldest son leaves home. She cried for an entire month, trying to cope with the separation.

Yogendra became the man of the house overnight after his brother had left home. He was in the 10th standard toggling his studies and responsibilities at home. Yogendra assured, "I promise you Maa, I will put in all my effort and hard work. I will not let my family down at any cost. I am sure I will produce more crops than our current production." Yogendra's mother was still unsure about Yogendra taking all duties upon himself. To his mother, he was still a child. Even his brother had been worried before leaving for the army. Jitendra felt nervous to leave his family behind and his brother managing all the burden. Before leaving home for Bhopal, Jitendra spoke to him, "You are now in charge of the house Yogendra. Please manage the work while I am away. I will write letters whenever I get time." The brothers did not express their emotions for each other easily but they cared deeply. Yogendra felt mixed emotions as his brother left home. On one hand, he would miss Jitendra's presence and guidance around him, and on the other hand, he was proud of his brother for joining the army.

His childhood was not like any other regular boy. Before leaving for school, Yogendra would get up early in the morning at 5 A.M and feed the animals. His mother would clean the shelters along with him. Yogendra would then go to the field and cut the sugar canes for his mother to later peel them. He would then bathe the animals and draw milk from the cows. Yogendra then got ready to attend school at 8 A.M. School would get over in the afternoon. Yogendra came back home and left for the fields immediately after lunch. He would have the assigned duty of cutting the canes in the machine after her mother left the peeled ones on the field. After the by-product was overloaded, Yogendra would have to put them in the crusher. His life was bound in a fixed routine. This taught him patience and discipline which was necessary to keep calm and repeat tasks every day. Often it was hard to maintain the same enthusiasm but Yogendra kept pulling through. While his friends played and ran around the fields, Yogendra worked in the field. There were a lot of sacrifices that he had to make for everyone. He had his family to look after and also complete his tasks.

Yogendra had a huge burden on his shoulders but he gave his all. He worked all morning in the fields, trying to match his brother's efforts. Heat and rainfall could not deter his motivation. His young growing muscles put in every ounce of strength to pull the plough through the fields. Yogendra would equally balance the housework and his studies. For a fifteen-year-old boy to tackle such big tasks was surprising and commendable. He managed to keep the promise that he had made to his mother. That year they had produced more crops than any other year. Yogendra's mother was proud of his determination. He had negated all her doubts and fulfilled his responsibilities with accuracy. When Yogendra's brother came home for the holiday, Jitendra was elated with the progress that Yogendra had made. Things had only become better at home and the farm.

Jitendra was relieved to realize that his brother would be able to handle problems in his absence.

When Yogendra turned sixteen, people in his class had already started applying for the Indian Army rally. His friends had also persuaded him to send his application. Yogendra did not think he was of the proper age to join the army then as he had recently been promoted to the eleventh standard. He wanted to apply for the army after completing his schooling and giving the higher secondary board exams. People made several attempts to get selected in the army. Therefore, Yogendra's acquaintances simply wanted him to try as chances of selection on the first attempt were slim. Yogendra, however, was completely sure that once he gave in his application, he will put in all his effort and get selected. His confidence did surprise many of his friends. Some may even have regarded it to be ignorance or overconfidence. Some of his friends even joked, "Do you think all seats are vacant for you?" Yogendra did not pay heed to any of their words. He had trust in his abilities and intentions to achieve a goal in life. His mother shared the same belief. She was sure Yogendra was headstrong enough to get selected in the army. She was against this decision as she had already seen one of her sons depart for the army. If Yogendra got selected in the army, he would only be able to come home once every six months. Yogendra's mother did not want to be separated from another son for so long, therefore she wanted him to join the police force. This desire, however, did not turn out to be true as Yogendra had already made up his mind.

Since his childhood, Yogendra had always imagined joining the army and becoming a soldier like his father. Yogendra had seen his father and his friends sharing their stories. They would all sit in a group near the house, smoking hookah and chatting about their days in the army. Yogendra was enchanted by those stories. His father shared his experience of taking part in the Indo-Pakistan War of 1971 as a sepoy. The recollections included his unit reaching Lahore during the war. He narrates the misery and pain of losing fellow soldiers and friends. Food and drinks become a prized possession in such harsh conditions. Yogendra's father recalls, "The taps available for drinking water had been poisoned by Pakistan's army. I watched my team members die in front of my eyes, choking on the poison. Yet we did not give up and kept moving forward." Yogendra absorbed these stories discussed in the group. He would be a silent listener taking every word in and building his own imagination. These stories did not scare him away, rather they inspired him to serve his nation. The wartime stories had created such an impact in Yogendra's mind that he would often see it in his dreams. These dreams became stronger when Yogendra was merely fifteen years old. In his dreams, Yogendra would always imagine himself in the military uniform. This vision provided him immense joy and motivation.

Jitendra encouraged Yogendra to apply for the army rally. Jitendra's shared his training experiences in the army which heightened Yogendra's interest. He convinced a few of his friends and together they decided to go for the examination in Meerut BRO. When the young boys reached Meerut, they were informed that they would first have to pass the physical examinations. The physical assessment was a piece of cake for Yogendra who had been spending hours on the field, building his core strength in the most natural way. They easily passed the test and left for home the next day. Yogendra's mother was not at all surprised to hear about his selection in the first round. She rhetorically inquired, "You are not going to stop anymore, are you?" Yogendra could only smile and confirm his statement. Within 15 days, Yogendra was summoned for the medical examination which was also cleared with efficiency. The final round was the written test. Many local brokers and agents approached Yogendra offering to clear his examination and finalize his admission in exchange for money. They tried several tactics to convince and entice him but Yogendra was not willing to walk on the incorrect path. Although Yogendra was an average student in school, he wanted to choose the honest option. Yogendra was confident that he would be able to pass the test on his own merit and he did. In a month results were out and Yogendra had been selected in the Indian Army.

Yogendra had passed his written examinations in November 1996. Soon after on 26th December, he was asked to report at the

Meerut BRO. When he reached Meerut, there were twenty-one other soldiers along with him who were informed that their training center would be in Jabalpur. Yogendra had hardly seen any other place apart from his village. Delhi was a completely new city that he had not explored. Yogendra had only visited Delhi once with his mother during his childhood. The memory was then distant and non-relatable. On 27th December, all twenty-one soldiers were put on a train for Jabalpur by commanding officer Colonel R.K. Singh. He directed the soldiers, "You are a soldier now. You must not fear anything around you but respect every individual. You must maintain your discipline and behaviour at all times. However, also have the spirit to answer back to anybody who insults the nation or the army. Remember boys a soldier is never afraid, he is the cause of fear among the vile." With that mantra in his mind, Yogendra started his journey for his destination The Grenadier Regiment Centre, Jabalpur.

II

'Gurukul'

Late in the night, Yogendra and the other soldiers reached Hazrat Nizamuddin railway station. They waited all night for the break of dawn. In the morning, after asking around, they got to know that the train towards Jabalpur leaves in the afternoon. When they reached Jabalpur, a bus was already waiting to take them to the army centre. As soon as they sat on the bus, Yogendra felt the already present butterflies in his stomach start to flutter voraciously. He had been counting days to get to the camp and wear his uniform. It was then only a matter of a few hours. In no time the bus reached the centre. All excited soldiers rushed down the steps of the bus. Jogendra was in awe as he looked around the huge campus. This was going to be his home for the future. Yogendra was one of the youngest in the lot aged sixteen years and five months. There was constant chatter among the people trying to figure out the place and know about each other.

They did not have to wait for long as one of the officers came to address them. People around were already informed about the arrival of the soldiers. When the officers had heard that the soldiers were from the Meerut BRO, some of them chattered, "Oh! This is the bus of the rebels. Something is surely going to happen." Yogendra then learnt that their camp had been infamous for causing mischief. The officer in charge ordered, "Come on, take out the knives that you have in your bag?" Yogendra was taken by surprise. He had no idea what the officer was speaking about. He could not comprehend why someone would carry knives to the training centre. As others whispered, Yogendra learnt that some rebellious boys would commit such improper acts and then they would be disciplined by the seniors. This is why there was generic information regarding their recruitment centre. Yogendra felt bad about the generic remark as he would never do anything to break the code. When it was time for his bag to be checked, he softly whispered to the officer, "Sir, I think there is a wrong impression about us. We are here to follow all rules." The officer smiled and replied, "It is a protocol soldier. We have to be careful at all times."

The soldiers were then escorted towards the dining area for breakfast. After their first meal, they had to complete the documentation process. Initially, they had thought that all twenty-one of them would remain together in the same team. However, soon they were divided into groups of four and five and sent to different companies. Yogendra was paired up with four other soldiers. All the new faces were gradually becoming acquaintances. After the formalities, five of them walked together for lunch. This is where Yogendra started a conversation with one of his group members Amarjeet Singh. Instantly, the two fell into a comfortable repertoire. Amarjeet was a tall, muscular Sikh boy from Delhi, about two years elder to Yogendra. During lunch, they spoke about their hometowns and families. All the members on the table spoke to each other. They were all interested in knowing the people they were going to live and learn with.

Lunch had hardly ended when a man walked into the cafeteria. His presence could hardly be ignored. Yogendra learnt that the tall man with a large moustache was an 'Ustaad', a non-commissioned officer. He walked to the centre of the room and his voice boomed around, "Listen to me heroes, I want all your beautiful silky hair cut by tonight. You may play with your lovely hair until then for the last time. You must look like a soldier by the end of the day." Although he had a humorous tone, the seriousness of his statement was clear to everyone. Some boys who had long hair were a little sentimental about losing their possessions. All the soldiers were called to the corridor. They stood in a queue waiting for their turn. Yogendra watched the lightning-fast abilities of the barber. Amarjeet, being a Sikh was saved from the process. Yet he was there to support his friends or so he promised. As soon as a soldier sat on the chair, the barber drew a circle around the edge of the hair and then quickly spread his knife to bring it to a proper crew cut. The soldiers laughed and made fun of each other's hardly existing hairstyle. Yogendra was not spared by Amarjeet making silly faces and adding to the mockery.

After dinner, the new joiners were ready to end the day. They had to get good rest for the early start the next day. However, things did not go as planned. Hardly had they entered their dorms when they heard the whistles blowing in the dining room. Yogendra and others were informed that the whistle meant that they had to assemble immediately. The meeting was called by the senior soldiers. As soon as they entered the dining area, all doors were locked. Yogendra could feel the palpable silence. Completely unsure about this call, all soldiers felt nervous. One of the leaders ordered, "Lie down on the floor boys. Do you see the pieces of *chapati*? Keep crawling on the floor and pick up those pieces with your month." All the *ustads* had thick rods in their hand supervising the drill. Some were subjected to the sting of the rods. Yogendra did not imagine such a warm welcome on the first day. Amarjeet huffed, "Is this the first day? Am I losing my memory?"

After hours of the excruciating activity, the senior soldier suddenly remembered, "Does this group also consist of the new soldiers who joined today?" Everyone answered in affirmation. The senior spoke again, "I had completely forgotten about the new joiners. Nevertheless, it's done now, so all of you pay attention to my next words. We have all come here for the food. All our hard work and efforts are for the sake of our survival. How is it then that the same food is being disrespected by all of you? Does not matter if the food is undercooked or overcooked. You have to pay your due diligence to this privilege that you have received. If you had been respectful towards the food, you would not have to take the punishment. Henceforth, I expect all of you to give importance to every grain that you are graced with." Yogendra learnt a life lesson on that day that he never forgot. In life, he had never again left food on his plate as he felt grateful for the boons which were provided to him by time. Destiny decided what a person gets in life and Yogendra understood that when your necessities are fulfilled, one must treat it as the best and be appreciative.

As soon as the soldiers woke up in the morning, they were given their khaki uniforms for training. For the next two days, they were familiarized with the drill grounds, offices, and other areas of the campus. From 6th January, Yogendra started his zero week at the training camp. By then the soldiers had been provided suitcases, blankets, and mosquito nets. Initially, Yogendra had been worried about the money but the seniors had assured them that everything will be provided by the army center. They were given a shaving kit and were asked to remain clean shaved at all times. On the first day of zero week, Yogendra and his roommates woke up at 4 A.M. to enjoy the morning tea. Using a shaving kit was new for many, so they took their time relishing a good shave with the shaving cream. Soon the room was taken over by Ustads. The loud voice was still something they had to get used to. Ustad spoke, "Is this a vacation, boys? You are still busy shaving. Who is going to clean the room? The drill starts in five minutes." No sooner had his words died down, the thick stick made its presence felt. People started scampering in different directions. They quickly got ready and ran towards the drill area with their guns.

Luck was not in their favour on the first day. They were late for training by two minutes. The physical training instructor was ready with his punishment. They were made to do uncountable front rolls around the field. Yogendra was out of his wit like all other team members. As soon as they stood up, they fell to the ground due to their dizzy vision. Surviving the first day had been extremely difficult for all cadets. When they came back to the dorm, Yogendra identified the root cause of the problem – the shaving cream. They all decided that they would skip the shaving cream and quickly shave with water in the morning to avoid any delays. Amarjeet and all others agreed to

Yogendra's suggestions. They consoled themselves with the notion of using shaving cream only in their leisure time. However, there was no leisure for the troop. The next day onwards, they simply woke up and speedily prepared to attend sessions without having any time to look in the mirror.

Initially, the physical training was painful for all the cadets. Long hours were spent under the sun performing different exercises. Yogendra could hardly feel his muscles everyday after the drill. Amarjeet screamed in pain, "Brother! I don't know what sins I had committed in the past life." Yogendra would laugh at his friend's dramatic comments. He silently absorbed the pain, knowing well that their bodies were preparing to endure greater pains. Yogendra often encouraged Amarjeet, "Your body is going to become like iron, just as Ustad promises." Amarjeet laughed, "Firstly, the bones have to survive for it to transform into any other metal." Yogendra had found a great friend in Amarjeet. They shared a brotherly bond without which life in the camp would have been lonely. Away from their homes, the cadets found support among each other. They had become family for each other which was beyond the feelings of being team members.

Yogendra's training in the zero week also consisted of shooting practices. One morning all the cadets reached the ground and they were informed that they were to have shooting practice. They were given 0.22 riffles to shoot targets at a 50-meter distance. Yogendra watched as people were called one by one to shoot the target. He was nervous as he had never shot a gun before. It was Yogendra's turn finally at the end of the lot. He heard Ustaad call out his name and moved forward to take the position. He had picked up the gun before during drills but giving a test was a different feeling. His hands were sweaty yet he was excited to do the drill. People stood around and watched as Yogendra surprised everyone with his performance. Ustaad enquired, "Have you shot a gun before?" Yogendra shook his head in a negative response. Ustaad continued, "Well then it seems like you have a natural talent for it. The names of the cadets selected for the riffle team will be put up in while. You all are dismissed." Yogendra got selected for his accuracy along with some other soldiers. Although he was shooting for the first time, Yogendra successfully completed the tests. After being selected in the riffle team known as Young Blood ARA, the shooting practice kept becoming more difficult. Yogendra was still happy to be a part of the team as they did not have to perform regular drills and physical training. The riffle team was only responsible for shooting all day and perfecting their shots. Slowly they were given to shoot objects at 100 meters, 200 meters, and so on.

The phase of training had not been easy on any of them. Yogendra and his companions would spent hours in the scorching heat, their uniforms and bodies lathered in mud. On some days they would even have to continue drills in heavy rainfall. The ustaad's showed no mercy as they were focused on training the best soldiers. Yogendra was a diligent cadet, completing all tasks on time. Amarjeet on the other hand reminded him of the prankster back in the village. He was always looking out to have fun in between the rigorous training schedule. The cold weather and the recurring bruises on their bodies called out for drinks. Amarjeet, being the manager, would take upon himself to plan for a heist. The boys were aware that alcohol was stored in the pantry but the keys remained with the ustaad. It would be a great task to acquire the key but Amarjeet was not one to give up easy. Amarjeet gathered his team which consisted of Yogendra, Gagan and Venkat. They decided to start their mission after lights-out. Amarjeet slowly moved towards Yogendra's bed and tapped him, "Come on it's time." Yogendra quickly got up and saw the other two waiting outside their dorm. Venkat spoke in a worried voice, "If we get caught, we are going to get a huge punishment tomorrow." It was clear who the nervous one in the lot was. He was somehow forced to join by his other friend. Amarjeet encouraged, "Nothing will happen, Venky. Have faith in me." The other laughed at his brief motivational statement and Venky's expression which did not pronounce any faith.

Amarjeet took the lead and halted outside ustaads chamber. The man is usually a deep sleeper which was the only saving grace. Yet they had to tiptoe around and be very careful. Amarjeet whispered, "Guys, watch the corridor. I will go in now." He softly opened the door and entered the room. A huge form on the bed was still visible in the dark room from the mild light entering through the window. He thankfully did not have to search for the key as all his keys were hanging on the hook by the door. Tensed fingers or lapse in judgement led to the key dropping on the floor. The ones waiting out also got scared by the sound. It was so silent that even a little pin could have huge impact. The giant man twisted on his bed. Amarjeet felt sweat droplets on his forehead. He was ready to surrender right then. However, God may have been on their side as the man did not wake up. Amajeet gave out a huff of relief. He picked up the key from the floor and left the room.

The team waiting outside impatiently finally saw a ray of hope. The boys passed excited looks towards each. Without wasting any time, they moved towards the pantry. They had to wait behind the walls for the guard to leave for his refreshment break. Amarjeet had followed their routine for days before coming up with the plan. Venkats legs kept moving in worry and cold. Amarjeet scolded, "Stop making sound bro. Do you want to get us caught?" Venkat stopped his rapid movement. After eternal waiting, the guard did leave his spot. They only had a free window of five minutes within which they needed to get the job done. Yogendra and Amarjeet went inside the pantry while Gagan and Venkat waited outside to stay as guards. Amarjeet announced, "You know the signal boys. As soon as you see any movement, let us know." The duo went inside with their small torched. They could not risk switching on the lights. The cadets were quick. Yogendra supported his friend to spot the bottle of alcohol. Amarjeet picked it up in a flash and they were out. In no time they returned to their dorm without waking anyone else. The boys cheered to their successful adventure and enjoyed their warm night of sleep.

After six months of training, the cadets were finally allowed to go for leave. Everyone was excited to go back home. Yogendra had never experienced such longing towards his home. Returning, this time was completely different. The first holiday remained to be special for the rest of Yogendra's life. All cadets packed their bags and went their ways. Yogendra was going to meet his family but he was also leaving his new family behind. Amarjeet hugged Yogendra before leaving with the promise of meeting soon. Yogendra realized that he had made beautiful bonds in a short period of time and diverse emotions coursed through him. At the same time, Yogendra dwelled on the past bonds that he had to leave behind to join the army. Most cadets boarded the train together for Delhi. They had still not received their uniforms which would be delivered after the final ceremony. However, people still got interested in the group of tall and muscular men travelling together. Some thought they were sportsmen and started conversations. Train rides in India are usually filled with meeting strangers and getting to know them. All the boys went their separate ways when they reached Delhi.

Yogendra was excited to reach home and meet his family. All along the way, he felt giddy and it only kept increasing as he came closer to his village. He was anticipating meeting his mother the most. In the army, he missed his mother's tender love and care. When Yogendra entered the house, it was quiet inside. He knew his mother will be in the kitchen at that hour. Yogendra went in front of the kitchen door and called, "Maa?" Yogendra's mother was surprised to see her son. She quickly left the work and came to him to wrap her arms tightly around him. Yogendra was the closest to his mother at home. His mother cried, "Why didn't you inform us that you were coming? Your brother could have gone to pick you up from the station. You have become so thin. Are you not eating properly at the camp? I would have cooked all your favourites too." Yogendra laughed at his mother's blabbering, "I am not a child anymore Maa. I can come home alone and I am going to stay for a while so you can feed me as much as you want. Where is Papa? Okay, let me guess. He must be at the tea stall with his friends." Mother and son shared an inside joke about Yogendra's father's love for tea and a good chat.

Yogendra went out to look for his father and meet his friends in the village. To him, it felt as if he had been away for years. A nostalgic emotion coursed through him as he walked around his village. Over a few months, he had seen many changes which had also affected his character. He was more disciplined and responsible now and these changes also made him view things differently. As Yogendra neared the tea stall close to his house, he could see his father sitting with some of the neighbours and friends. Yogendra's father had a stunned expression on his which he tactfully hid. He was happy to see his son but his inexpressive nature did not allow him to portray those emotions. Yogendra touched his father's feet first, followed by the other elderly people sitting outside the tea stall. Yogendra's father inquired, "Was the ride back home comfortable?" He had very few words, unlike Yogendra's mother who had series of questions. Yogendra nodded his head, still very scared of his father.

One of the elderly men stood up and came close to Yogendra. This was a highly educated neighbour whom Yogendra admired for having knowledge and being trained in several languages. He started a conversation about Yogendra's training, "How are you doing son? How come you have come back so soon for the holidays?" Yogendra acknowledged the man with a nod, "I am doing great. I have been selected for the rifle team. So, we have been allowed to leave early for the holidays." The uncle was glad to hear Yogendra's reply, "Singh Saab your son has a spark. He is going to do something great in life." Yogendra's father laughed and commented, "I am not sure about that but we are happy that he has got a job in the army and that is enough for us." Yogendra stood quietly for a while, listening to the conversation about him. He then spoke, "Uncle my brother has gone for the technical domain but I am sure I am going to become a Havaldar before him. I am in the firing team and if I can perform well in the team within a year and a half, I will get the promotion." The elderly man recognized Yogendra's enthusiasm and encouraged him to work hard.

Yogendra spent the rest of his holiday helping his mother with farming. He did all the housework as he used to before leaving for the camp. Life back at home was peaceful. Yogendra enjoyed his mother's cooked meals and attention. He spent his time also chatting with his friends and telling them about the camp and his experience. He was relishing the pleasant break at home but at the same time, he was missing his friends and team members at the army camp. He would recall the training every night when he went to sleep. It was human nature to miss things we did not have. Yogendra knew he would be wishing for a break as soon as he returned for his job. Therefore, he wanted to relax as much as he could at that moment. When it was time for Yogendra to return, his mother could not control her tears again. She always missed her sons living far from home. He assured his mother that he would come back for the holidays again. Yogendra left home to return to his second home.

After Yogendra returned to the base, they were made to practice for hours on the shooting range. His hands would start to pain holding the heavy gun for hours. When they could not perfect the shots, trainers would beat them up with rods and cords. Physical pain was manageable for Yogendra as he had slugged in his village farm under terrible conditions. He did not break down from that treatment. He would accept all the punishment with a smile. Yogendra watched as his teammates would sometimes be on the verge of giving up. Their bodies would scream in pain as they hit the bed. They would help each other by putting ointments on their wounds and bruises. There was no mercy in the training as they were learning to face challenges. Yogendra found it more difficult to face the constant failure in the shooting practice. He made all efforts but could not achieve 100% accuracy. As time went by, the lack of success and encouragement diminished his interest in the shooting team. This led to him not being selected in the final core riffle team. By that time Yogendra was not upset anymore as he had made up his mind to move forward with some other skill. Yogendra had the quality of never looking back and he exercised the same at the crucial hour.

III
Coming of Age

Obstacles had always been a part of Yogendra's life. Not being selected in the firing team was only one of them. He had overcome his disappointment and put his mind to the training. Soon, there came another hurdle on his way. Ustad came into the dorm and called out, "Yogendra Singh, you have to report to the administration office immediately." Yogendra was scared thinking he might have made some mistake. As he approached the office, he was informed that the secretary was waiting for him. He stood near the specified desk and a man looked up from piles of documents, "Yes?" Yogendra cleared his throat and replied, "Yogendra Singh, Sir. I was asked to meet you." The officer fixed his glasses and stated, "Your verifications are incomplete, soldier. We are unable to reach your district office. You probably would have to go back home and get it done. Until then your Kasam Parade will be on hold. We will keep you informed regarding the issue." All cadets got their verifications successfully completed except Yogendra. Due to some logistics, Yogendra's verification was incomplete. This led to his final ceremony that is Kasam Parade get delayed. All his batch mates were getting certified while he kept waiting for his turn.

Yogendra was disheartened by the turn of events. Even Amarjeet had received news regarding his posting. He would crash the bed every day with the thought of officially starting his journey as a soldier. Around October, Yogendra was released for holiday for a week, during which he had to get his verification completed. Yogendra was somewhere relieved to go back home and get the work done by himself as he could not wait any longer. He was also mentally exhausted and being near his family would help release some of his stress. Yogendra felt more desperation than the happy jitters that he had felt while visiting home for the first time. When Yogendra reached home, he had another news waiting for him. His brother's marriage had been arranged and the date had been fixed in December. Yogendra's family was expecting him to return for the wedding. However, Yogendra knew it was impossible to get another holiday in two months. Also, he was going to get posted after his oath ceremony after which he would have to report for duty. Yogendra had very little hope of being back for his brother's wedding.

Yogendra's mind was only focused on the oath that he had to take in the felicitation ceremony. He went straight to the administration office as he reached the camp to complete his verification process. Yogendra could not wait anymore to join his batch-mates on the ground. He would often sleep at night and think about the moment when he would officially become a soldier and get to wear the uniform. His dreams as a child were close to becoming true. After Yogendra reported at the base, in a few days, he had his Kasam Parade. That morning was different from any other. To him, the sun seemed to be shining brighter than usual. Yogendra stood in the line with the other cadets while the Captain delivered his speech. Yogendra's eyes were fixated on the waving flag. His hands felt the texture of his uniform. He had never felt so strong and grand in his life. Yogendra took his oath with the other soldiers and meant every word that he spoke. He understood his responsibilities and knew that he could do anything for the love his nation. The sound of the bugles announced a new chapter in Yogendra's life.

All soldiers were assigned their units within a few days. Yogendra got posted in 18 Grenadiers. As stars would have it, Yogendra landed in the same unit with Amarjeet. The two friends had only been praying throughout their training period to remain together as long as possible. It seemed that their prayers were answered. Both of them were ready to begin their real journey as a soldier together. Amarjeet had become a brother for Yogendra and having him on his team was the best thing that could have happened. While he had one brother on his side, Yogendra could not be there for the other one at home. 31st December 1997, Yogendra received his official posting. His brother was getting married on 7th December. Yogendra's family was waiting for him to return. He received the wedding card from home which he took to the officials for requesting leave. His leave letter was rejected. This is when one of Yogendra's brother's friends came in to help. The man was in the U.P police and racked his mind to find a solution for Yogendra. He sent a telegram to Yogendra's base camp stating that his mother was in a critical condition. Yogendra was called by the officials soon after. He skipped through the corridor expecting some good news as the friend had asserted to him that the telegram would be quite believable and he will get the holiday. The first glance at the Ustaad's face told him that it was going to be the opposite. His limbs had turned cold and all the excitement had left his body. The superior had a knowing smile on his face and not the happy one. He inspected, "A few days back you had come with a wedding invitation card, right soldier? Now that your mother is ill has the wedding been cancelled?" Yogendra knew a trap when he saw one. None of the answers could save him from this situation, so he decided to remain silent. Obviously, the idea had failed and Yogendra could not attend his brother's wedding.

Before reporting for duty, the soldiers were allowed to go home for holidays. On January 1st, 1998, Yogendra went back home. He had to take the bus from Delhi, however, the buses were unusually packed on that day. Yogendra somehow managed to get inside a bus from Lalkuan with his heavy luggage. Yogendra lit a smoke and waited for the bus to depart. There was no empty seat, so he stood behind the driver's coach with his luggage laying on the side. Suddenly, he heard an old man call out his name, "Mr. Yogendra Singh?" Yogendra had never seen the man before, therefore, he was surprised by the encounter. Yogendra hesitantly inquired, "Do I know you, Sir?" The old man smiled and replied, "No son, I saw your name on your bag.

Where are you posted?" This got Yogendra into an easy conversation with the man, talking about their lives. The man seemed genuinely interested in and respected Yogendra's service for the country. Meanwhile, there was another person keenly observing the exchange. A woman was seated by the driver's coach with her eyes fixated on Yogendra. He was not sure about her inquisition and did not feel comfortable enough to question.

When the bus reached the stop, all passengers departed. Yogendra had huge luggage, so he waited for the bus to be empty. The woman by the driver's seat was still seated in her place. Yogendra softly requested, "Madam, please get down before me. I have a lot of luggage with me." The woman stared long and shook her head, "No, you must get down first" Yogendra was annoyed by the illogical persistence of the woman. His pathway was blocked by her suitcase. Yogendra patiently said, "Then please move your luggage, I need space to depart." The woman shook her head again, "I have no space to move either." By this point Yogendra had lost his patience, "I have no other solution. I will have to throw the bag obstructing my path." Not receiving any positive response from the fellow passenger, Yogendra watched her suitcase derail down the steps of the bus as he pushed it. There was weirdly no other confrontation between them. Yogendra hurriedly looked for an auto-rikshaw to get to the next bus stop to catch a local bus towards his village.

As Yogendra reached home in his uniform for the first time, his neighbours and friends applauded his success. His parents took pride in him officially joining the army. Yogendra had barely settled, when his mother insisted, "You must go and meet your sister-in-law. She has just got back to her house for a few days. She has continuously asked me to send you to her house if you return for the holidays by any chance. Thankfully you finally have time and you should meet her before you leave as you were not here for the wedding." Yogendra did not want to go alone as he did not know anyone at his sister-in-law's place. He conditioned that he would only go if he could take his friends and the car along with him. Yogendra avoided the topic for the rest of the week. He got busy with farming and his friends. This was going to be his only leisure time before he reports on duty. Once he leaves for the job, he would not be able to return home for a long time. Yogendra enjoyed his mother's care and relaxed in the calm atmosphere of his home.

One day while Yogendra was cutting sugar canes in the field, his mother called for him. When Yogendra entered his house, he saw a short, thin boy waiting by his mother's side. After enquiring, Yogendra was informed that the boy was his sister-in-law's brother. He was here to take Yogendra along with him to meet his sister and his family. What Yogendra could not fathom was how his sister-in-law came to know about his return. The young chap said, "My sister has requested you to visit. I am here to take you with me." Yogendra was not ready to go as the entire situation was awkward for him. He still insisted on his friends accompanying him which was not agreed upon by his family. After his mother's constant persuasion, Yogendra agreed to go under some conditions. Yogendra would only go if the boy takes him on his scooter and drops him back at his home within an hour. Everyone agreed and managed to convince him to visit the unknown household.

It did not take Yogendra much time to reach his sister-in-law's house. As soon as he walked through the entrance, he saw her entire family waiting in the living area. The surprise that awaited Yogendra was the girl standing beside his sister-in-law. This was the same girl who had a tiff with him on the bus on his way home. Then it clicked and all became clear. The girl was his sister-in-law's sister and she was the one who informed her about his arrival. The girl had not seen him at the wedding but was aware of his name and also Yogendra looked like his elder brother which made it easier for her to guess. The girl was still staring at Yogendra, "Did you recognize me?" Yogendra nodded his head, feeling uneasy with multiple eyes on him. The girl teased, "Were you trying to break my leg with the suitcase?" Yogendra had to defend his honour, "You were not moving. I had already warned you." The entire family had a good laugh as they narrated the story of the encounter. Yogendra gradually became comfortable as the family warmly welcomed him. He had lunch and conversed with all the family members.

Within a few days, it was time for Yogendra to leave for his posting in Kashmir. His family knew that Yogendra was not coming back anytime soon. His mother broke down in tears, "Son, promise me you will take care of yourself and you have to write to us regularly." Yogendra was the closest to his mother. He could not bear to see her crying. With lumps in his throat, Yogendra promised, "I will. You must not worry too much and take care of your health. I will be back before you know it." Yogendra's father put his hands on his head as a sign of blessing and wished well for his son. Yogendra's brother embraced him, "Don't you do something stupid and die on us now." The brother shared laughter which was a rare sight. Yogendra was always afraid of his elder brother and had never joked with him. The relationships were certainly becoming more eased as Yogendra grew older and became a responsible adult leaving to serve his nation.

IV
Boot Camp

On 7th February, 1998, Yogendra reported for his posting in Jammu. In three day, the unit was called to the Srinagar transit camp, Badami Bagh Cantonment. After spending two days at the camp, they left for the Corpse Battle School in Khrew. Yogendra was placed in the 5th Platoon unit. When he entered the camp, officials were relaxed. It was bone shivering cold for he had never travelled to the mountains. Due to this cold weather, as was the rule alcohol was being circulated among the soldiers. As soon as Yogendra stepped inside the common area, he was spotted by an Ustaad. The tall man approached, "Hey boy! When have you arrived?" Yogendra replied, "I have just reported on duty Sir." Ustaad nodded and ordered, "Alcohol is being issued. Go and get me two drinks in your name." There was no saying to no to a senior. Yogendra was used to his seniors' wrath, so he did not take any chance and walked towards the counter with a glass.

One of the senior officials was pouring out the drink at the table. People had queued in front him and Yogendra waited for his turn. When he reached the front of the line, the official noticed the lean boy standing tall. The office enquired, "What is your name? I have not seen you around. When did you arrive?" Yogendra replied, "Sir, Yogendra Singh Yadav. I have just arrived." The officer raised his eyebrows, "Oh you are in a hurry boy. Ready to fetch alcohol after two minutes of arrival? Don't you feel ashamed?" Yogendra stood there without another word. The officer continued, "No, I do not think the drink is for you. You have surely been sent by some Ustaad to get more alcohol." Yogendra could not have revealed the truth for he knew his life would become difficult at the job if he did. He mustered up confidence, "No Sir, it is indeed for me. No one has sent me." Yogendra tried to convince the official and get out of the place. The official doubted, "Have you had alcohol before?" Yogendra smiled and replied, "Yes Sir, I have been drinking since the sixth standard." The official was surprised to hear this, "Really? Isn't sixth standard too small? How did you get alcohol?" Yogendra answered, "My father is an ex-army official. So, he would get the alcohol on quota. We would sometimes drink from his stock." This might have convinced the official, "Alright, I will give you three drinks but you have to drink it in front of me." Yogendra agreed and chugged down the alcohol. As he was leaving the room, Yogendra was stopped by the ustaad waiting for his drink. Yogendra apologized, "Sorry Sir, I could not get your drink. The official did not let me leave with it and asked me to drink it in front of him." The Ustaad was surprised to hear Yogendra, "You drank all that alcohol?" Yogendra nodded his head which resulted in a pat on his back and shared laughter.

After a month of rigorous training at the Cantonment, Yogendra got inducted into the Kashmir Valley with the 5th Platoon. The training at the centre had been different from what they had previously learnt. Apart from the physical combat training they were also being skilled in strategizing and interacting with terrorists considering they would have multiple encounters in the mountain. They had to learn to interrogate militants and special tactics of attack. Yogendra's experience in the mountains was nothing like he had seen before. There were tall pine trees lining up the roads and mountains. Yogendra's eyes filled up with all the greenery around him that beautifully blended with the white snow. The snow laden peaks had mesmerized the young mind. The cold weather did take some time to adjust to. They huddled up around bonfires, their only relief in the bone-chilling cold weather. Working with his fellow soldiers gave Yogendra the opportunity to learn new things. Every soldier received the chance to establish their identity and evolve into better versions of themselves. Yogendra did not have exceptional skills of strength or intelligence when compared to others in his unit. All soldiers were equally fit and able at their task. What made Yogendra special was his humble nature and the zeal to achieve more. Yogendra was the youngest soldier in his Platoon. He would wake up in the morning and prepare tea for everyone. He treated everyone with equal respect and in return he received the same. Yogendra completed all chores in the unit before being directed or orders. He would clean the camp are and fill drinking water in all pots. His forthcoming nature had attracted the attention of his seniors. The entire team continued to train in special combat tactics and interrogation skills. They were continuously being prepared to face terrorists and deal with such situations.

The Platoon continued operations around the valley for eight months. However, they failed to locate any militant activity. June 1998, all battalions were detailed for the Amarnath Pilgrimage. The companies were segregated and allocated different tasks. Yogendra's unit was managing the Sangam location at the very top. The view of the entire world from the top was completely different. Things seemed minute to Yogendra in front of the infinite nature. The isolation from the common life and people raised multiple thoughts in Yogendra's mind about life and existence. The only companion apart from the unit was music. The symphonies floating in the air united them all. The lyrics of the songs seemed to establish their meaning even more in that lonely valley. Yogendra's eyes traced the snowflakes falling on the empty land non-existent of humans, animals or plants. They sat for hours listening to the soft sound from the radio. Once Yogendra had asked his senior, "Do you like listening to music alone?" The words of the senior made home in his heart, "Music reveals its true meaning in isolation." Yogendra understood and absorbed the true feeling of solitude in the mountains.

In ten days the pilgrimage had begun and the pilgrims started to flood the area. The unit had to walk fourteen kilometers from the base till the top daily in three hours of time. These round trips for the entire route had to be conducted twice or thrice each day. They even had to help pilgrims and carry luggage all along the way. After the Amarnath duty, Yogendra was granted leave for a month. The holidays went by in the blink of an eye and Yogendra could not wait to return to his unit. When he returned to Srinagar at the end of July 1998, he was informed that his battalion had reached Kupwara. Yogendra and some other soldiers were waiting in Pattan for the convoy to take them to Kupwara. Finally, they got hold of a government transport and started their journey. They had a senior official with eleven years of service and all other young soldiers in the bus. The senior directed the driver, "Inform us when we reach Kupwara. We have to go to Lolab valley." It was a beautiful journey on the snow laden roads. Some tired souls had fallen asleep on their seats. Yogendra looked outside the window enjoying the scenery and losing himself in his thoughts. The driver may have been equally lost as he missed the stop. When they had almost reached Trehgam, the driver suddenly remembered, "Where did you say you had to get down?" The senior replied, "Kupwara. Are we there?" The driver spoke in a hurry, "We have passed Kupwara long back. We have reached Trehgam." All soldiers were worried about not being able to reach the camp on time. They instructed the driver to halt the bus at Trehgam. Without wasting time, the senior official requested the C.M.P officials on the Trehgam post to call and inform the Major at Kupwara about the happenings. Major Devgoda commanded the soldiers to spend the night at Trehgam and informed them that a vehicle would be sent in the morning to take them to Lolab Valley.

As promised, the next morning all the soldiers were taken to their destination by Army Vehicle. As soon as they reached the camp, Major Devgoda was there to welcome them and not so warmly. His voice rang loud, "Were you boys planning to go to Pakistan?" The young soldier had their eyes stuck to the floor. Yogendra spoke up with some courage, "No Sir. We were in the government bus and had informed the driver to drop us at Kupwara. There may have been some miscommunication and he missed the stop." The Major scanned the room filled with silent observers, "Give your explanations to the Commanding Officer. He wants to meet you all." Major Kushal Chand had recently joined as the Commanding Officer of the battalion. Yogendra and the others were going to meet him for the first time. Yogendra was certain that this would not be the best first impression. They entered the office and watched the well-built man standing with a stern gaze. All the soldiers could feel sweat droplets on their forehead even in the cold weather. There were no introductions of warm welcomes. Major enquired, "Why are you here? Do you know your purpose?" The question was directed towards all but the senior official became the primary target, "Sir, we are here for the operations." The Major took a step forward towards the group, "Operation? Are you a doctor?" They were well aware of the sarcasm and the question was not to be answered. The Major left the room after a loud announcement, "Subedar, take care of this bunch." Yogendra knew about the care that awaited them. The cold hard ground waited for them to perform uncountable front rolls. The weather was not on their side and the light drizzle and hard ground stole the essence of the combat uniform.

Search operations started soon after and the team was on high alert. They conducted around twenty-five operations within a short period of time with a great success rate. Yogendra's first encounter with a militant was in November 1998. Yogendra had gone home for his leave. As soon as he returned, he was informed that they had to leave for an overnight operation in Kupwara. Yogendra had not received the opportunity to pick up his snow boots before the operation, so he had worn his regular boots. All night they remained outdoors in the snow, patrolling the area. Next morning the wet boots had lost their shine. As expected, Yogendra was called in by his supervisor, "Who is going to shine your boots soldier?" Yogendra explained, "Sir, I had been out for an operation all night. My shoes are still wet." Yogendra knew well that all explanations were excuses and they were not accepted. The superior nodded, "Alright no problem. You will be carrying the rocket launcher today to our destination. We have a new operation." There were no questions asked and Yogendra was ready for the punishment.

The battalion had to travel to a small village in Manasbal. They had received an intel from a villager of ongoing militant activity. Yogendra had to walk the entire distance with his AK 47 and the rocket launcher which came up to sixteen kilos of weight on his shoulder. They had to cover a distance of twenty kilometers by foot. Yogendra had a hard time walking with the burden on his shoulders, however, he was not one to complain or give up.. When they finally reached the village, the villagers were asked to evacuate the area. The army always had to be prepared for the worst outcome, therefore extra measures had to be taken for civilian protection. The mosques were used as the announcement centers. They were all surveying the area and preparing to take guard. One of the officers was repeating instructions, right when the first bullet hit the walls. Soon bullets flew all around them like heavy downpour. Loud noise and dust blanket had engulfed them and Yogendra had never experienced anything like this before in his young life. For a moment, everything seemed to be running at high speed. Yogendra needed time to process but he had none. All soldiers were in the same fix and the only savior was their survival instinct. The soldier ran as fast as they could and took cover behind several houses.

The Second in Command had taken charge of the situation and the only solution to prevent the attack was announced, "Get me the rocket launcher." Yogendra was still in possession of the large mass. His ustad's voice rang in his ears, "Run with the rocket launcher and give it to the officer in charge." Yogendra screamed through the noise, "Sir, I don't know how to fire this." Ustad did not wait and began tying the material on Yogendra's back, "You won't need to do anything. The 2IC will take care of it. Just reach there alive." Some distance had to be covered to reach the pit where the officer had taken cover. The constant firing made it difficult for one to maneuver. Yogendra had to be quick and alert to avoid the bullets. When he started to run along the distance, his company provided cover with constant shooting towards the enemy camp. Somehow, Yogendra reached the pit alive which at that point had seemed like the most difficult task. The officer in charge took the ammunition from

Yogendra's hands, "Soldier, do you know how to fire this?" Yogendra shook his head, "No, Sir." The officer took his position and prepared, "No worries, let me show you how it's done." Yogendra watched an entire house blow up in the distance and the firing stopped. They had assumed the bullets to be travelling from a certain direction and shot their missile in that direction. After the firing had stopped, the unit had searched the entire village but could not find any of the terrorists. They had already changed positions and escaped before the rocket launcher had been fired.

In the evening, they all sat behind a house strategizing and talking about the event of the day. Two of their men were surveying the area and walking around the village. They came across a multiple paddy straw on an open area close to their pit. They began poking and removing the straws to look within. The first two piles had nothing suspicious, so the soldiers continued their search. It all happened in the blink of an eye. Yogendra saw men dropping to the ground from the corner of his eyes. In an instant, all soldiers picked up their guns and fired in the common direction. One of the militants had been hiding in the huge pile of straw. When the two soldiers found him, he immediately shot them. They had not expected a charge and dropped dead on the ground. The militant got shot in his leg as the unit fired at him. He, however, did not give up and ran towards a short fence and jumped over it. Even in that moment, Yogendra could not help but learn from such determination. The terrorist was aware that he would not survive this day but he refused to give up. He ran with his numbed leg and all his strength. As soon as he jumped over the fence, he was shot by the soldiers guarding the other side. Yogendra understood that every individual teaches us an important lesson, both our friends and enemies.

This was the first near death experience for many of the soldiers, including Yogendra. They had lost two of the soldiers of their team. Things had suddenly become too real and the harsh reality hit them hard. Some were too shaken up to witness the transience of life. The bodies were covered and transported to the base. Yogendra kept thinking about the lifeless bodies of his fellow companions.

Yogendra's Ustad noticed his faded face, "What happened, soldier? Are you alright?" Like many others in the company, he had taken a liking for the humble young man. Yogendra pretended to be better than he was feeling, "Yes Sir." The Ustad knew that all soldiers needed time to absorb the event, "Death is the ultimate destination young man. We are all headed towards it. The only difference is that a soldier's death has a meaning. We all sacrifice our lives for the country and having the tricolor wrapped around our bodies is an honour." Yogendra found reassurance in these words. He was here for the love of his country like all others. They will have to be prepared to face death at any hour and so will their families. Instead of fear, Yogendra found more determination to avenge the death of companions and protect his nation.

The next day, the unit continued their search around the area and found two militants. The streak followed in the next month and they completed many successful operations. The unit became fierce and challenging after the death of their men. They were all brothers and it felt like losing their own family members. They were ready to take out all terrorists in the area at any cost. They achieved a difficult feat by killing Babar, who was the area commander and a wanted individual. During that month, Yogendra encountered the dark and wicked face of terrorism and its impact. The villagers were either always scared of the terrorists or following their path. People were beaten and tortured to death and they had no way to safeguard themselves. Women and young girls had to face molestation and rape. The militants terrorized the people so that no one could revolt against them. Young teens were continuously manipulated with the notion of religious ideologies to join the terrorist organization. The seed of hatred and animosity towards the nation and people are sown in the young mind which grows into huge, dangerous roots. Yogendra realized that fighting against one's own countrymen was far more difficult than other countries.

V

Adversities

December, 1998 was spent through many more operations in the valleys. Radio communications established that President Atal Bihari Vajvai had appreciated the peaceful relations between India and Pakistan. As things were running on a lighter note, the new soldiers were asked to leave for the holidays by order. They were sent for two months of long leave. Company Commander Major Rajesh Adhikari had to approve the leaves before the soldiers left. Although the leaves were by order none of the soldiers revealed that they were instructed to take their leaves. Yogendra was questioned by the Commander, "Why do you need two months of leave?" Yogendra, like all other soldiers, lied, "There is no particular reason Sir. It is too cold in January and February, so it would be good to join in March when the weather is better." Commander was not convinced, "So what if your marriage gets fixed? You are going to again ask for leave after you return." Yogendra smiled and shook his head, "No Sir, I have no plans of getting married anytime soon." Despite having doubts, Yogendra's leave was approved by Major Rajesh. Yogendra left for home, not knowing how true the Major's words would turn out to be.

Yogendra had returned home after a long time. The parents were delighted to see their son safe and secure. The news of attacks on the valleys had them worried at all times. Although Yogendra wrote often to let his family know about his well-being yet seeing him in flesh and blood was a welcomed relief. Yogendra's mother spoke, "Son, I am so glad that you are back. You have become so thin. Now you must eat well and rest for two months completely." His father only shook his head from the lawn chair that he had occupied. Yogendra laughed at his mother's statement, "You only see me becoming thin, mother. I am absolutely fine." His mother was ready with a reply, "Fine is not good enough. You need more care and attention for your health. We have discussed it, your father and I, you should now settle down and let someone take care of you." Yogendra truly did not have this in his itinerary. He did not think he was of the age to get married and his job did not make it any easier. However, he knew reasoning with his parents would be pointless. So, he simply nodded his head and left for the farm. Yogendra knew it takes time to find the right girl and finalize things. He had hoped that it would soon be time for him to return on duty and the entire agenda would take a backseat for a long time.

Indian arranged marriages mostly consist of relatives bringing information regarding eligible brides and grooms and parents short listing the some candidates. The next step includes parents going to the eligible woman's house and then making their choice. Yogendra's house was handling the first phase. Relatives, friends, and neighbours were bringing multiple 'rishtas', however, none measured up to the expectation of his parents. Yogendra was not very involved in the initial phase. Months went by with daily meetings and discussions in his house. People came to his house daily to talk to his parents. It was almost nearing the end of his vacation yet there had been no good news for his parents. Yogendra, on the other hand, was slightly relieved that he would escape the marriage riot this time. He could not wait to be back at the base with his fellow companions. Luck did not favor him for long. Almost at the end of his vacation, Yogendra's parents found the ideal match. His father and elder brother went to the would-be in-laws house. They liked Reena at the very first instance when they saw her. She was calm and gentle and exceptionally talented. All her qualities made her the right match for Yogendra.

As was common in arranged marriages in the era, Yogendra did not meet Reena before the wedding. He had only seen her picture. The decision made by his parents was the final one. He did not mind because he knew his parents would make the right choice for him. Moreover, he liked Reena for her photograph. In a generation, when virtual reality had not overpowered social interaction, Reena's photograph somehow portrayed her simplicity and grace. This did definitely convince Yogendra that his parents were on the right track. It was time for Yogendra to leave and this time was no different for the family letting their son go. The only ray of hope was that he would be back soon in May for his wedding. The first thing that Yogendra had to do was to report back to Company commander Rajesh Adhikari, "So, soldier, is there anything you would like to spill?" Probably his expression revealed a little more than he had intended. Yogendra replied, "I am getting married in May, Sir. It happened all too soon. My parents found the right girl and decided on the dates." The Major had a knowing smile on his face, "Didn't I tell you this is what was going to happen?" Yogendra answered, "I did not plan for it, Sir but I will not need a long leave. Twenty days would be sufficient."

Yogendra had not even spoken to Reena after their wedding date had been decided. However, opportunity did present itself for them to meet. Yogendra's senior in the unit was getting married to Reena's friend. He was invited to the wedding. When Yongendra's father heard about this, he called him, "Son, go and meet her. This is the opportunity. You would at least get to see the bride before the wedding day." His relatives also spoke to him and encouraged him to go and see the bride. Yogendra's mother was, however, not in favor of this, "This is against our rituals. The groom does not meet the bride before marriage in our culture. I do not want you to go, Yogendra." He could never defy his mother's command. Yogendra loved and respected his mother the most. He was the closest in the house to his mother. Therefore, he decided to not go for his friend's wedding and meet Reena. There was a lot more calm and patience in that generation. There was no hurry as he trusted his parent's decision.

Yogendra became busy as soon as he reported back on duty. Things were moving fast as multiple operations were lined up. They found some leads and followed them through but none of them turned successful. Until one day they received an intel from one of the young village boys. With a lot of difficulty the boy had reached out to Major H.P Singh. In a distant village in the outskirts of Kupwara, a terrorist group had been conducting meetings in a closed school. They had been manipulating young boys in the name of religion and trying to bring them on their side. Some of the boy's friends had already been convinced by the theories of the organization and had been attending the meetings regularly. The boy came to know that they would be given basic training in combat to defend themselves from the army. However, the real agenda was to conduct a mission with the help of these young lad. The boy did not know what they were planning but it had to be something big. Too naive to identify the real motive, most boys had been swayed by the idea of protection and prosperity.

The team was urgently briefed and prepared to raid the run down school in the middle of the night. The convoy dropped them at a distance. The soldiers had to cover the rest of the way by foot. The school was surrounded by a pine forest. The soldiers walked through the dark and dense forest. Yogendra felt the silence pierce through their ears. The mist in the air did not make it easier for them to maneuver through the forest. Major H.P. Singh was in command of the operation. They neared the old, broken walls of the school, taking cover with every step. Vision was compromised as the only saving grace was the moonlight. They had to be very quiet to avoid any firing from the opponents. Major signalled for the soldiers to spread out and enter through different directions. They could easily detect activity in one of the rooms on the ground floor. A soft bulb lit the room. There were four men sitting around the fire. With one command from the Major, they attacked the men. They were not prepared to counter and were easily taken down. However, this was just the beginning as suddenly there were many more men firing at them from the first floor.

The soldiers scampered around to take guard behind the pillars and desks. One of them shot the bulb to provide them some leverage in the dark. Yogendra was waiting behind a small cabinet in the room. He had almost stopped breathing for even the slightest movement made a loud noise in the silence of the room. Everyone waited for the opponent to make a mistake and the firing to begin. They did not have to wait for long as one of the militants stumbled over a glass making his position known. Bullets flew in that direction continuously. The unit started approaching the stairs as some militants ran to the first floor. Yogendra and two other soldiers followed behind the Major towards the eastern wing of the building. Major Singh commanded the two other soldiers to check one of the two rooms while Yogendra followed the Major into another room. Major Singh ordered, "Be alert soldier and remain behind me." He knocked the door open with a kick. They began to survey the room together. It appeared to be empty in the first instance. Then suddenly a bullet came out of nowhere. Yogendra, instinctively, shot in the direction of the firing and a terrorist dropped down behind the desk.

Yogendra turned to see the Major lying on the floor. He had a wound above his stomach. There was a lot of blood but the intensity of the injury could not be accessed. The Major tried to speak but no words could be comprehended. Yogendra kneeled on the floor and put his hand over the open wound. He attempted to calm the wounded man, "Sir, do not try to speak, please. You will be fine." Yogendra was appalled to see this powerful man struggling in pain. The other two soldiers came into their room when they heard shots being fired. They took the Major to the ground floor as soon as they got the signal that the area was clear for evacuation. By the time they could have taken Major Singh to the hospital, he had taken his last breath in the vehicle. Yogendra and the entire unit was shaken by the incident. To them it felt like losing a guardian. Major Singh had always directed them well and been in the forefront in all operations. Even his final operation had been successful. The company stood around his casket as the Commander said some words in the honour of the Major. With the queue from the Commander, the soldiers fired their shots in the sky. Yogendra was not afraid of death but losing his own men hit him hard every time. It also made him determined to put all his effort into future tasks. The company conducted many more successful operations in the coming months. Terrorist units were taken down one after another. The men were all charged and there was no stopping them.

In between his busy schedule, Yogendra had no time to ponder upon another important matter in his life, his wedding. Before he could get time to process, it was already the end of April. Yogendra left the camp and reached home on 1st May. His family was ready with all the arrangements. As soon as he reached home, he was given several instructions. There was the 'tilak' ceremony that had to be conducted in the evening. Yogendra had to quickly get prepared for the event. A new pair of traditional kurta and pajama had been laid out neatly on his bed. Soon, his brother came calling for him as his in-laws had arrived. Yogendra was meeting his in-laws for the first time. There were a lot of people gathered in their courtyard. People were sitting around the 'havan' and the 'pandit' prepared for the 'puja'. Yogendra was introduced to all his in-laws one after another. He went ahead and touched their feet to get their blessing. According to traditions, the bride did not attend the 'tilak' ceremony. The groom had to get the blessings of God and all his elders before his wedding. Yogendra sat beside the pandit and followed all instructions provided by him. He repeated the 'shlokas' narrated by the pandit. Soon after his forehead was marked with the 'tilak'.

After the culmination of the 'puja', Yogendra's father-in-law blessed him and presented him with gifts. The entire family was given new clothes, sweets and fruits. Yogendra's parents had also prepared for the ceremony. They not only blessed their son with a gift but also presented gifts for the bride and the in-laws. The entire evening was spent in laughter and merriment. Music was being played by the aunts and grandmothers. There was a huge arrangement of delicacies for dinner. Yogendra had never seen such a celebration in his house as he had been absent during his brother's wedding. He was glad to be with his family for a while as there was very little time for him to spend with them. Also the lights and flowers did momentarily take him away from the lonely darkness of the pine forest and the ice cold winters. The next few days followed with many more ceremonies. Yogendra had even jokingly asked his brother, "Why can't we straightaway get married? Is this constant torture necessary?" His brother had come up with a witty reply, "Brother, this is just a drill. It is teaching you to prepare to deal with difficult situations after marriage." The brothers shared a good laugh over the banter. Yogendra still respected his brother immensely, however, the fear had subsided somewhere as they became more mature.

Finally, 5th May was the day of the wedding. Yogendra had been in intense situations during his operations, however, this event did in fact make him nervous. This was going to be the beginning of a new journey and he would become responsible for another life. The car had been beautifully decorated for the groom. After some final traditions and blessings from his mother, Yogendra went on his way with his family. As soon as the groom's car reached the premises of the bride's house, loud music could be heard. People began bursting crackers and dancing to the tune. Yogendra was welcomed by his mother-in-law. She blessed him along with Reena's aunts. Everyone gathered around the entrance excited to see the groom. Yogendra was escorted by the bride's family. They were doing everything possible to make him comfortable. Soon the pandit began chanting his 'mantras' and Yogendra repeated them diligently. The bride joined Yogendra after a while. This was the first time Yogendra saw Reena in real life. Yogendra could not steer his eyes from his bride. Everyone admired Reena for how beautiful she looked in the attire of a bride. Yogendra believed that the photograph had done no justice to Reena's grace.

The wedding was a beautiful event for both the families. Everyone showered their blessings as the bride and groom took their 'pheras'. The lavish feast followed after the wedding. Yogendra's friends enjoyed themselves with drinks and dancing. The time of 'vidai' was the most difficult for Reena as she had to leave her family behind and start a new phase with Yogendra. They said their goodbyes and left for Yogendra's home. Yogendra's mother was ready to welcome the new bride with multiple customs. Once all traditions were completed, the bride and groom were left to rest. Yogendra and Reena did not say much to each other that night. They were shy and needed time to get to know each. Both were tired and slept on their sides and slept on the opposite sides of the bed. The next day they had their reception ceremony conducted by Yogendra's family. Many of Yogendra's friends from the army attended the event. Even Amarjeet came all the way to support his friend on this grand occasion. The entire week went by in fun and gala. There were a lot of rituals to follow which Yogendra could not keep a count of. He did whatever made his mother happy.

Yogendra and Reena did not get a chance to go on a lavish vacation, however, they managed to take a day trip. Yogendra's mother had insisted for them to visit the Ganesh temple far from their house right after their marriage. Yogendra, as always agreed to his mother's wish. They started their journey early morning. Reena had not been to many places outside the town. She was very excited to visit the temple. Yogendra could sense this excitement from her eyes that were constantly focused on the passing view from the window of the bus. It took them five hours to reach the destination. Yogendra got themselves sweets, garlands and incense sticks for the 'puja'. Reena walked beside him inside the temple. The priest accepted their basket and asked for their names for the ceremony. The priest blessed the newly married couple after the 'puja'. Yogendra asked Reena, "Should we go somewhere and eat?" Reena nodded her head, still very shy to speak. They went for lunch at a vegetarian restaurant near the temple. The couple remained silent except the occasional questions about the food. Suddenly, Reena started coughing and Yogendra grew concerned. He quickly placed the glass of water near her lips. Reena drank a large gulp from the glass and their hands touched over it. Taken by spice and concern the couple did not notice their initial contact. As both problems subsided, the young couple moved away, too embarrassed to look at each other. Yogendra enquired, "Are you alright?" Reena nodded her head again. Reena liked Yogendra's concern and learnt about his attentive and careful nature. On their way back, the couple also realized how comfortable they had been in each other's company where conversation did not need to be forced.

In the meanwhile, Yogendra also came to learn more about Reena. She spoke very little but her actions rang loud. Reena took care of everyone in the house and Yogendra liked that the most about her. He learnt that Reena liked to listen to music in her spare time. Yogendra would often play the radio loud while Reena was working in the kitchen so that she could hear it. They eventually became friends, talking about their childhood and home. Yogendra would tell her about Kashmir, his friends in the army and catching terrorists. Some of the stories would scare Reena and some made her laugh. Yogendra loved to hear her laugh so he would avoid all serious details in his stories. They had the simplicity in their relationship that made it strong. Reena also learnt to analyse Yogendra's moods and habits. As time neared for Yogendra to leave for duty, she mentally prepared her for the separation. Before marriage, Reena was well informed that Yogendra was a soldier and half his time would be spent away from home. His life is full of dangers and he would have to always risk it for the nation. Reena knew all of it and was prepared mentally, however, her heart would still ache from time to time with the thought of Yogendra away from home.

Few nights before Yogendra was about to leave, he woke up from a terrible nightmare. Rubbing sweat droplets from his forehead, Yogendra went for a walk in his courtyard. Seeing her son up so early, Yogendra's mother approached him, "What happened? Why are you awake?" Yogendra's pale face did tell her something was wrong, "Maa, I had a nightmare. I could not sleep anymore." Yogendra's mother pat the stool beside her, "Come sit by me, son. Tell me what did you see?" Yogendra replied, "Maa, I saw some men running away with our national flag and our soldiers were chasing them. There was a lot of firing on both sides and our soldiers were dying. I feel something is really wrong." Yogendra's mother patted him, "There is nothing wrong. You are always around militants, so these thoughts are common for you. Don't think too much about them. Come on, you only have a few days left of your vacation." Yogendra listened to his mother's words but the negative feeling in his gut did not subside.

19th May came around and it was time for Yogendra to leave. His parents were getting used to the idea of him leaving. Reena, however, was experiencing the separation for the first time. Yogendra could not fathom the difficulty she would be having in dealing with the situation. Yogendra was closing his bags when Reena entered the room, he called out to her, "Hold this. You should buy something with this." He gave her a 100 rupee note as a parting gift. Yogendra continued, "When I come back next time, I will get my salary and I will buy you something more. Until then you can use this." Reena nodded her head. Both did not know how to say their goodbyes. It was just recently that they had begun to know each other and it was too soon to part. As Yogendra was about to leave the room Reena softly said, "Take care of yourself. Eat on time and keep yourself warm." She quickly slipped a locket into Yogendra's hands. He opened his palm and looked at a small 'ashtadhatu' locket of Lord Hanuman. Reena said, "You must always wear this locket. This will keep you safe." Yogendra smiled and nodded and asked her to take care of everyone. He told her to learn Matar Paneer dish from His Mother ,as this was the best dish he loved to eat . He took the final blessings of his parents. Yogendra hugged his mother trying to capture the warmth in her embrace, the memory of which would comfort him in the cold. He waved at everyone and walked out of the door, not knowing when he would return.

VI

Enemy is at the Door

20th May, 1998, Yogendra reported on duty in Jammu. After Yogendra submitted her documents, he heard an announcement. It was notified that the soldiers of 18 Grenadiers would be sent to Srinagar in the morning by a convoy. When they asked around, the soldiers came to know that there was terrorist activity spotted in Dras, in the Kargil district. Soldiers were being moved to the region to defend and stop the attack. Yogendra recalled his nightmares and the feeling in his gut strengthened. 21st May the soldiers reached Srinagar and on the 22nd of May, Yogendra reported in his unit's base camp. Amarjeet had also reached Srinagar on the same day. The Subedar informed them that they would not be joining their companies who had already left for their operation. They were required to help out the Charlie and Delta companies who did not have fighting porters. Each soldier had to carry 25 kgs of ammunition up the mountain path to the units fighting on top. They would work the whole day, non-stop to continue to provide resources to the forces. They continued to walk for twenty-two days straight.

The only means of communication was the radio which told them about the attacks on different companies fighting in different directions. Amarjeet and Yogendra were sitting at the base having their food before starting their journey back on top. They were lost in their thoughts listening to the radio news in the background. Suddenly, they heard noise in the distance. When they looked up, they could spot some activity in the distance. Both of them became alert with their guns as it could have been militants. As the men came closer, Yogendra noticed that it was their own unit. They identified men running with a stretcher. The worst thought came to their mind and usually it was real in the valleys. Yogendra moved towards the unit to check what was happening. The men had dust all over them but one of them had blood on his hands and clothes. Yogendra asked, "What happened? Are you hurt?" He moved closer to check and his eyes landed on the lifeless body of his teammate on the stretcher. His mind connected the dots. There was gloom all over the faces of the soldiers. The soldier on the stretcher was Ravi Dikshit. Yogendra had trained with him in CBS. He saw a bullet wound on Ravi's forehead.

Yogendra could not hold on to his anger anymore. Watching his companion die in the hands of the terrorist was the worst feeling for him. His veins popped as he heard the other soldiers, "There was a lot of firing from the top. Visibility was almost zero. We managed to take guard as soon as the bullets flew our way. Unfortunately, Ravi was hit by then. We decided to retreat as the opponents had a vantage point and we did not have any further plans." Yogendra imagined every hour what he would do when he received the opportunity to face his enemies and avenge the death of his mates. He counted days and waited for his turn. The beautiful mountains and trees on the valleys did not allow one to imagine the horrible happenings on the top. Only the sound of artilleries could notify one that there were constant attacks going on in the mountains. The silence and beauty of the mountains stood in stark contrast with the ugly bloodshed and deafening bombings. Yogendra could not fathom who would want to spoil such a beautiful nation and these thoughts only made him angry with the militants.

The news of casualties and deaths kept escalating as days passed. Yogendra came to know that the team led by Naik Subedar Lalchand was totally wiped off. Also a team led by Subedar Randhir Singh from the alpha company were killed. The entire team of twelve members were brutally murdered. This news made Yogendra's blood boil. The constant fire of revenge burnt in his heart. It also pained him to think about the companions that everyone had lost. Yogendra had still not received the chance to use his rifle to end the enemies. During this time, he again had an encounter with Major Rajesh Adhikari. Major recognized him, "Soldier, you have come back?" Yogendra nodded his head. The Major continued, "Why did you return? You shouldn't have." Yogendra smiled and answered, "Sir, my holiday was over. I had to come back." Major enquired, "So, did you get married?" Yogendra nodded again. Major repeated himself, "Oh! That is great news. You shouldn't have returned. Things are not great here." Yogendra replied, "Sir, I would have come back at any cost. It is my dream to fight for my country. Finally it is going to be fulfilled." Major Adhikari smiled at the lad's enthusiasm and left with a gentle smile and appreciation.

Major Adhikari took air shots of the area on that day. Soon, three helicopters were sent to survey and shoot in the marked locations. Yogendra and the other soldiers were climbing the mountain in the evening when they heard the sound of firing. They looked up in the sky and noticed the helicopters in the distance. Had it not been an attack, one could admire the synchronized movement of the choppers and the setting sun in the background. The helicopters quickly fired and turned to move in the other direction closer to the climbing unit. Two helicopters had surpassed the targeted area. While the third one had taken a turn, Yogendra watched it go up in flames. A huge ball of fire covered the distance in the air and landed on the helicopter. Within seconds, the entire chopper was on fire. All the soldiers stopped their movement and stood in place to look at the happenings. It all occurred so fast that everyone needed a minute to process the event. People were still looking up at the sky to figure out what happened to the chopper. However, the outcome of that fire was quite obvious. The helicopter had crash landed somewhere in the forest. The soldiers had to be careful with the next steps as they were unsure what lay ahead.

After the incident of the helicopter crash, the team was informed that the Bravo Company would be conducting an attack on the same day. Major Rajesh Adhikari was leading the team to the top. When Yogendra heard about the plan of attack, he was hopeful that they would become successful. He had met the Major and had grown to respect his abilities. The entire day as the soldiers walked through the steep path, Yogendra kept thinking about Major Adhikari and his team and their progress. When they completed a round trip and reached the base, the environment in the camp was silent. People's faces were faded and there was a palpable tension in the air. Yogendra asked around like the other soldiers in the team. As soon as Yogendra heard that the mission turned out to be unsuccessful, his heart dropped. The worst news followed, Major Adhikari and his entire team had been wiped off. Yogendra could not believe that the man he had met a few hours back was now dead. He was an excellent mentor and guide and Yogendra knew it was a major loss for all of them.

In the earlier operations, the bodies of the dead soldiers could be retrieved as they had dropped at a distance from the enemy base. There were entire teams brought down and bodies sent to families for the final ceremonies. Major Adhikari's team was the first one who had been able to enter the enemy camp and were killed there. There were nine members in the team and not a single body could be accessed. The other companies could not go near the enemy base where the bodies were lying. The families had been informed of their death but the bodies were yet to be recovered. The companies were planning attacks from different directions but the constant firing did not allow them to go near. Yogendra's mind wondered about the families waiting to see their son for the last time. To not be able to complete the last rights for one's child would be the most painful for families. Even the army wished to honour their martyrs for which they tried all measures possible.

In the meanwhile, right after the attack on Major Adhikari's team, on 22nd May, suspicions were raised about the attacks. Initially, the attacks were considered to be conducted by the terrorists. However, with more attacks and deaths it was becoming clear that the Pakistan army was involved in the attack. Major Adhikari's data had also pointed to the fact that such a huge parameter could not be covered by a terrorist group and also the intensity of the attack was high. The speculation was continuously circulating among the soldiers and the media had also started picking up its sources. Yogendra heard the news over the radio and wondered why the neighbouring nation would plan such a terrible attack when things had been going great. Even the Prime Minister had announced previously about the friendly relationship between the nations. The countries had been planning several events to promote peace and solidarity. This act of betrayal breaks the new formed base of trust and enrages the harmonious nation.

Next day, the team was guided by a pahalwan from the Charlie Company. While Yogendra's team was ready to climb through the set route, the pahalwan advised, "You must take the other route. There are more shootings on this path." The team followed the instructions and completed the climb in daylight. The team was happy about the quick progress. They reached the top by 4 P.M. and the Havaldar was constantly by their side. After a few minutes of rest, they began their ascent down the mountain path. Soldiers were talking to each other about the news of the day. Yogendra watched the Havaldar trail along the route. He enquired, "Sir, what are you searching for?" Havaldar spoke softly, "Nothing specific. Just keeping an open eye. It's not safe anywhere these days." Yogendra nodded and kept walking by the huge muscular man. There was some assurance felt while walking beside such a figure. They had covered almost half the distance when suddenly Yogendra noticed that the Havaldar was not by his side. Yogendra looked around and called out for the man. He then noticed that Havaldar was left a few steps behind. As Yogendra approached him, he noticed that the man was looking at something on the ground. Others had also stopped walking and looked at the object. Everyone was inquisitive to know the issue.

Yogendra questioned, "Sir, what are you looking at?" The Havaldar answered, "It is a broken piece of artillery." Yogendra did not think much of it as it was nothing unusual to find in that zone, "It is a used one, Sir. We should move ahead." The Havaldar insisted, "Wait soldier! Let us inspect this a bit more and then we can go." Yogendra did not pay much attention to the words. As he started taking a few steps towards the base, the other soldiers had also followed. Yogendra did not think there was any point inspecting that object, therefore, he left the Havaldar to look at it by himself. As they took 20 steps ahead, a loud voice followed, "Oh man! I am dead." The entire team was on alert. Yogendra knew instantly that the voice belonged to the Havaldar. The team had just seen the man and then his painful shriek was shocking. Yogendra, along with the other soldiers, rushed back and noticed that the bulky man was down on the ground. His hand clutched on to his legs and his lips only parted in pain. The Havaldar was lying on an open space and he did not have any guard. Yogendra rushed near the man and pulled him towards the bushes. Immediately, a bullet rushed past the area where the Havaldar was lying down. A sniper had been hiding in the bushes ready to shoot. Had Yogendra been a second late, the lively man would have been dead.

Yogendra had previous encounters where he watched his companions being shot down. The men dropped dead immediately after they were shot. Hence, Yogendra had not experienced their screams of pain. Here there was this strong, stout man screaming like a child as blood oozed out of his leg. Yogendra could not fathom the amount of pain the man was enduring. Yogendra thought to himself, it is only when one is shot, can they feel the intense pain and suffering. Havaldar screamed, "I am going to die. This pain is unbearable." Yogendra was not sure but it appeared that the bullet was still lodged inside the thigh. Havaldars body twisted on the ground in pain. They had to get the bullet out before the leg got infected. Carrying a man with 100 kgs of body weight was not an easy task, especially when they are writhing in pain. The soldiers were confused as to how they were going to pick the Havaldar. When they tried to move his body, very little movements were giving him a lot of pain. Finally, they decided to carry the man in their waterproof cape. Four men held the cape on each side. Every time the cape shook, the Havaldar's scream pierced their ears.

Yogendra decided to hold on to the Havaldar's leg to keep it straight. He figured this might lessen some of the pain from the frequent jerking. It took more time than usual to get down from that difficult route. Base was already informed about the injured man. The ambulance had to be called to send Havaldar to the hospital. When the team ascended, they noticed that the ambulance was already waiting. Yogendra felt relief to have successfully completed the task of bringing the patient down and getting him the treatment that he would require. The team quickly started their upward journey again. They had to spend their night on top of the hill. The team usually spent their nights and rested on top of the hill. The base camp was an open location and could be easily identified. Sleeping in the mountains gave them the opportunity to protect themselves and remain secure. The soldiers would only come down to the base during the day when cars came to drop ammunition and other resources.

When the soldiers reached back on top, they were all famished. One of Yogendra's senior ordered, "Yogendra, you are going to stay up tonight." One of the soldiers had to stay awake all night to guard the area if anything went wrong at night. Yogendra enquired, "Why me?" Everyone was tired and so was Yogendra. He had been awake for the previous night as well. The senior replied, "I do not feel too well. My body aches." Yogendra did not want to defy his senior, so he quietly accepted the command. It was not very difficult for him to stay awake as his thoughts hardly let him sleep these days. The nightmares were true and his nation was in danger. Someone was trying to harm the national flag and all that he had mysteriously seen made sense. He wondered if his mother was seeing the news and what she would be feeling. He had discussed his nightmares with her before he left home. His father would probably be consoling her while she worries her heart out. Yogendra imagined whom Reena would be confiding with. She spoke so little and was new to the household. This must all have been so terrible for the families worrying about their children every night. However, Yogendra knew this was the price to pay for the duty he had chosen. His love for his nation came before any of the other relationships in his life. Yongendra, with his eyes fixated on the constellations, remained lost in his thoughts.

VII

One Steps at a Time

The dead bodies of Major Adhikari and his soldiers could not be retrieved. Yogendra's mind kept circulating on this fact. He imagined the emotions of the families and that enraged him even more. There was also a feeling of sadness for losing brothers of the nation. Yogendra's interactions with Major Adhikari had always been interesting. Even at such a high post, the man had been humble and down-to-earth during all his communications. Yogendra leant a lot from his personality and behavior. Both men were fond of each other which was evident from their occasional interactions. Yogendra could not but forget their last communications. Even then the Major had only wished him well for the new chapter of his life. Yogendra continued to feel blessed to have met such a man and been in his company. His heart was resilient and mind was made that he would fight with all his heart to avenge the death of these brave men who sacrificed their lives for the nation and the families who lost their children to unfair fate.

Second in command, Lieutenant Commander R. Vishwanathan planned another attack on 2nd June to rescue the dead bodies of the soldiers. There were rigorous meetings and plans were chalked out to reach the enemy base. Commander Vishwanathan led his team to the top. They slowly took time to access the area and not make any mistakes. The team was already alert about the enemy waiting to kill them from their vantage point. The tall trees on the mountainous path were the only support for the soldiers. The climb was not easy and death lurking in the air made it even more difficult. The soldiers relied on constant commands and words of motivation from the Commander. The team had been located by the enemy as soon as they neared the base. Every movement was easily visible from the base at the top and nothing the Indian soldiers did could erase that disadvantage.

Within the blink of an eye, bullets rained on the soldier from the enemy camp. Lieutenant Vishwanathan quickly threw out orders and tried to tackle the situation. There was a lot of commotion and soldiers were running around to take refuge. The Second in Command could not be stopped by the fear of bullets. He kept moving forward with all his might. He had almost reached the base and enemy faces were visible to him. Just when Lieutenant Vishwanathan looked at the enemy faces, suddenly a bullet plunged into his belly and two more followed. Commander Vishwanathan's body dropped to the ground. Lieutenant's radio operator immediately informed the Commanding Officer Khushal Thakur, "2IC has been hit, Sir." The news came as a shock to the Commander. He instinctively ordered, "If you can see him, pull him down right now." The radio operator put all his strength and grabbed onto the Lieutenant's leg and dragged him to a safer location. The man was still conscious and fighting. His spirit was not ready to give up although his body was incapable.

Just as the Commanding Officer was listening to the radio communication, he could feel the bullet rush past him and hit his operator's head. He watched the lifeless body drop to the ground and blood gushed out of his head and filled the ground beneath. He collected himself and ran towards Lieutenant Vishwanathan carrying his own radio set. Apart from being team members, they were great friends. Commander dropped to his knees beside the Lieutenant, "Vishu, you are going to be alright. You must stay strong." He could sense life seeping out from his friend's half-closed eyes. Lieutenant Vishwanathan's shirt was soaked in blood and the color had turned to a blackish-green. He tried to speak but words came out feebly, "I do not think I will live." His words shook the Commander but he knew he would not be able to lie to the Lieutenant. The dying man continued, "We were continuously being informed that there is a group of 10 to 12 terrorists at the top which is completely false. There is a deployment of Pakistan's army with huge ammunition and strength. Our entire team would be wiped off and we would still not be able to uproot them in this manner. We need urgent artillery support and reinforcement to drive Pakistan's forces away."

The Commanding Officer reassured him and watched in amazement as even in his final minutes, the Lieutenant worried not about his life but his country. The spirit of a soldier projected the indomitable strength and determination. People around could not help being anything but proud of his sacrifice. They fulfilled his final wish of speaking to his wife. Lieutenant Vishwanathan cleared his shaking voice, "Meenu?" His wife could have recognized that voice from anywhere, "Vishu? Are you alright? Your voice sounds different." Lieutenant Vishwanathan smiled at his wife's endearing habit of asking multiple questions at a go, "Yes, I will be fine. I have less time, so listen to me, please. Take care of Amma and Appa and yourself. I love you, Meenu." This is all the strength he had and his body went limp. A voice called out his name from the other end of the phone but the Lieutenant was already gone. The Commanding Officer picked up the phone and gave out the official information. Loud screams and cries filled the vacuum in the air. All soldiers felt helpless in such moments where they had to inform the family of their dead brothers. Yet they consoled themselves and the others to remain strong and keep fighting.

The entire team was struggling through a phase of demotivation. When Yogendra and the other soldiers came to know about the death of Second in command, Lieutenant Commander R. Vishwanathan, they lost their morale. Yogendra was disheartened by the news of losing two great leaders consecutively. The team had lost almost thirty-five soldiers and officers. The planning, however, did not stop. The officers at the higher levels constantly chalked out strategies. No one was ready to give up yet. Yogendra and the other soldiers in charge of transporting ammunition were not aware of the planning at the higher levels. They simply did their daily tasks and waited for the orders. Yogendra was in anticipation of being called to actively fight for the death of his companions. Within three days team 2 RAJRIFF had joined Yogendra's team. They had started climbing and transporting their ammunition. Yogendra could feel that backup was being prepared and soon there would be some action.

On June 12th evening, Yogendra and his team were completing their daily climb when they witnessed a huge artillery fire. The dark evening sky filled up with orange balls of fire. The bombs pierced through the white ice on the mountains and fire spread everywhere. The sight was equally beautiful and dreadful. Yogendra's eyes filled with the colors of fire and his heart mimicked the same. The porter team had no prior notice of the attack being planned which is usually organized by the leaders. They heard the loud noise of the bombarding and started to guess the strength of the ammunition. Suddenly, there was a surge of energy in the team, trying to figure out the plan of action. There was an increase in hope as they watched additional support arriving for the team. The soldiers then only wanted to kill the enemies and avenge their dead. The artillery firing continued throughout the night. This led to the successful capturing of the Tololing peak by 2 RAJRIFF at 8am on 13th June. Tololing was an extremely important location for the army as it could overlook the vast expanse of Srinagar - Leh Highway.

Although Tololing had been captured through joint effort, there had been no individual victories for the team of 18 Grenadiers. 2 RAJRIFF retrieved for another mission after capturing Tololing. To motivate the soldiers of his team Commanding Officer of 18 Grenadiers, Colonel Khushal Thakur encouraged, "Soldiers, the next point is going to be captured by us at all costs. Are you ready?" All soldiers screamed out their affirmations. The energy was still high from the previous victory and the Colonel wanted to use the surge of this saved energy. The company had to quickly change their location from Tololing. The planning was underway and the soldiers were preparing for the final orders. Meanwhile, the soldiers managed their tasks of organizing their ammunition and preparing food. The word was already out that they would have to move any minute. Some final minutes were spent taking of rest and having meals. Yogendra was walking past when Amarjeet called, "Brother, come and have something. There will be no time once we start moving." Yogendra replied, "Save some for me. I will just fill the waters and be back."

The soldiers were all scattered over the area, completing the final packing. Some were sitting in groups around the fire. They were about to start their journey towards the top. Suddenly, a huge mass of artillery dropped on the group of soldiers sitting around the fire. The Pakistan army was already aware of the troops capturing Tololing. As they had the advantage of knowing the location of the Indian battalion, they did not waste any time in their attack. The impact was so huge that the others walking around crashed on the ground. Yogendra was walking with a filled pitcher in his hand when he felt the ground being swept from under his feet. His body was pushed to a distance from the impact. The loud deafening noise of the artillery took him into a trance. He could only watch bodies on the ground. As he got oriented with his surroundings, he saw shadows running around. His eyes then traced the location around him and it landed on the dismembered bodies of his teammates. Minutes ago his friends were laughing around the fire and then some heads, hands, and legs were scattered around it.

Yogendra instantly remembered Amarjeet sitting in the same place waiting for him. He got up from the ground and started frantically searching for his friend. Yogendra prayed to not see the familiar face on the ground. There was a lot of smoke around them and all soldiers were in a hurry to evacuate the area with the casualties and the dead. It was difficult to maneuver in the dark with things haphazardly thrown in every direction. Yogendra had to look carefully on the ground to not step on any of the bodies. He somehow found a torch and looked around minutely. The light hit a spot on the ground and Yogendra's throat became dry. He was familiar with shining object that reflected the light. He went closer to look at the bangle attached to a severed arm. Yogendra immediately knew it belonged to Amarjeet. He had forever watched his friend wear the religious bangle (kadaa) with pride. He removed the bangle and walked ahead with the hope of finding his friend maimed and not dead.

Yogendra's optimism failed as he took two more steps in the dark. No one else could have identified the burned body in the haze. However, Yogendra knew his friend. Amarjeet was face down on the ground with very little left of his body yet somehow miraculously his turban remained in place. Yogendra dropped to the ground and clutched the tattered body of his friend. Tears rolled down his cheeks and words could not escape from his lips. Yogendra had never felt such intense pain in his life. To him it was like losing a family which he had never faced before. Memories flashed in front of his eyes from the days they had spent together at the academy. Many scenarios started playing in Yogendra's mind with multiple what-if. He even blamed himself for not asking his friend to come along with him for the menial tasks yet he knew that there was nothing he could have done. Yogendra was extremely proud of his friend who lost his life as a martyr on the battle ground, serving the nation.

Yogendra felt extreme anger and pain coursing through his body. It had felt miserable to lose his leaders and companions along the way but it felt even more personal losing his friend. Somehow the desire for revenge strengthened in his mind. He needed one chance to prove himself and serve his country. At that moment, Yogendra tried his best to remain calm and focused, however, it became extremely difficult while he packed his friend's dead body. They had lost about seven soldiers on that day. On the mountainous terrain, it took about six to seven people to bring one soldier to the base. It took them long hours and about hundred soldiers to bring the bodies to the camp for them to be sent to their families. Yogendra could have never imagined carrying his friend's lifeless body with his own hands. It had been the most difficult journey for Yogendra until that point in time. He could not fathom the news reaching Amarjeet's family.

18 Grenadiers had lost members of the family and that drove them towards the idea of immediate revenge. Yogendra was still working in the porter team. Another division from the battalion had been prepared to attack on the enemy front on the same day. The soldiers were charged to kill the opponents and take over the peaks. Colonel Khushal Thakur led his team towards victory. They used the advantage of the darkness in their favour. While the enemy was expecting the company to be still managing the bodies of their martyrs and recovering from the drastic attack, the Indian army lodged their improvised attack. The soldiers carefully crawled up the mountain and avoided making any noise. The enemy's ignorance was their power. Night vision glasses guided the soldiers on the path towards enemy bunkers. It was more difficult to crawl on the rough and steep route with the heavy artillery on their back. The enemy was taken by surprise from the sudden attack. The Indian soldiers easily pinned the Pakistan's army down while they remained distracted.

Overnight, Humps 1 to 7 were captured by the battalion. Radio communications reached Yogendra and the other soldiers of the team. This was the first big step for their battalion. Yogendra could only imagine the emotion of watching the Indian flag being hoisted on the peaks. This was a major success for the Indian army. It was a moment of hope and pride to watch the tricolor float over all the seven peaks. After the victory, the entire team of 18 Grenadiers was ordered to withdraw and come back to the main base camp. The next round of wars were led by the 13 Jammu and Kashmir Rifles. The entire Indian army came to know about this huge win and this only encouraged every battalion to continue their fight with equal rigor. The soldiers of the 18 Grenadiers had descended by orders although they wanted to continue to the very top. It was a strategic decision made by the high command to allow other battalions to follow next with fresh energy while the existing troops could recover from their wounds from the battles.

The soldiers had gone through hell and back during their stay in the Dras region. Their faces had changed drastically and they could hardly recognize each other. All soldiers had big beards and bruised faces. Extreme sunburns had blackened their skins while severe humidity and cold cracked their cheeks and lips. They had lost count of the days that they had not taken a bath. They could not certainly go into civilization in this condition. After numerous days, they finally got to shower and clean themselves. They shaved their beards and cut their long hair. When Yogendra stood in front of the mirror, a familiar face looked back at him, however, the eyes told him something had changed. The soldiers not only had to tend to the physical wounds but also the mental trauma that they had to endure. Yogendra had seen death before, however, losing a loved one changed something within him. He could only feel the change but could not identify the difference. His heart was still aching for his friend but there was also a calm acceptance. The calm definitely provided him strength in the miserable hour to maintain hope and courage.

After spending a few days at the camp, the soldiers were eager to get back in action. The news on the radio informed them about the victories of different battalions in the war zone. Yogendra was eagerly waiting to fight actively with his fellow companions. Just as the soldiers were becoming restless to return, a meeting was called by Colonel Khushal Thakur. All soldiers of the battalion sat inside a huge tent waiting for the Colonel to address them. The Colonel's voice rang inside the tent, "Soldiers, 18 Grenadiers have been asked to report back. We have been assigned the task to capture Tiger Hill. This is an honour for the battalion to receive another chance to fight for the nation and avenge our own." The soldiers cheered when they heard the news. This is what they had all been waiting for. The Colonel explained the plan in detail. Every individual in the team was briefed about their duties and also about the tasks assigned to the others. Every minute detail was briefed and it was made sure that people had clarity about the plan.

They had multiple sessions in the day to train them mentally and discuss the progress. The backup plans had also been clarified. Colonel did not want to take any risks with this attack. He wanted to capture Tiger Hill at any cost which would automatically help them to win the war. Colonel Khushal Thakur announced, "We are leaving for the battle tomorrow. We have to make our army and the nation proud. We must do everything in our power to achieve this. Are you all ready?" The entire battalion of soldiers cheered out loud. Colonel Khushal Thakur continued, "Come on boys, let us show them who we are. Sarvada Shaktishali." The war cry echoed in the mountains as hundreds of soldiers screamed with conviction.

VIII

Think before You Leap

Strategies and plans continued for the next few days. The team leaders traced the area and locations on the sand models. The Commanding Officer's usually briefed the team leaders about the duties on those models. The team leaders then explained the plans to the soldiers. Yogendra and the other soldiers simply listened to the instructions and tried to memorize them. There could be no mistakes made and for that they needed to be on the same page. Yogendra continued with his daily tasks at the camp. The soldiers mostly spent their time keeping themselves fit and practicing combat. Yogendra continued to gather respect from his companions and seniors and he kept being noticed for his humble and forthcoming nature. He took up extra chores at the camp and always completed them quickly with efficiency. Without his knowledge, people were already observing and appreciating his qualities. Having time on their hands, Yogendra simply wanted to keep his mind and body busy.

All soldiers had to physically recover from the bruises and mentally heal from the stress. Yogendra was also experiencing similar trauma. He could hardly share his experience with anyone. Yogendra mechanically went about work trying to distract his mind from the raging thoughts. One of the nights Yogendra twisted and turned in his bed. His teammate the other Yogendra, accompanying him since the academy days in Meerut sensed the restless movement. Singh (Yogendra 2) watched his friend soaked in his own sweat. His lips parted to whisper the feeble words. Singh could only hear Amarjeet's name which sounded like a cry for help. Singh shook his friend's arm watching him writhe in distress. Singh spoke in a calm voice, "Wake up Yogendra. You are fine." Yogendra's body shook like a tremor and his eyes opened expecting a scary sight. When he noticed his friend sitting beside him, he calmed down. Singh enquired, "Are you okay?" Yogendra nodded and replied, "Yes. Just a bad dream." Singh patted him on his shoulder, "How long have you been having these nightmares?" Yogendra wiped his face with his palm, "Since Amarjeet..." Yogendra did not need to complete the statement. The entire company knew about their friendship. Singh assured, "I know no one can take Amarjeet's place. He was a great soldier and he has given his life for the nation. We need to honour his death and fight for his revenge. You have got me by your side and you can talk to me whenever you need."

The turmoil in Yogendra's heart would not settle overnight, however, his companion's words brought him some peace. Nothing could change the void in the hearts of the soldiers that had been created from the deaths they had experienced. With the sadness, there was also anger and resilience in their minds. Yogendra thought of revenge every day. He wanted to kill every individual whose hands were the cause of the death of his brothers. Yogendra often thought about the journey he had taken together with his fellow soldiers climbing the mountain every day. They would sometimes lose heart to keep on continuing. All the soldiers encouraged and motivated each other to not give up. Yogendra found strength in his father's words whenever he felt disheartened, "Son, the person in front can only move ahead if they receive support from behind. Therefore, you should never stop and give all your effort." Yogendra drew motivation from these words and even when people got tired, he continued to push them. All the soldiers counted on each other to complete their mission.

Yogendra did not consider his task to be of less importance than the others. He knew that without the support from the porters, the soldiers will lose the fight. They need the ammunition and other resource to put up a brave front. Therefore, Yogendra believed his team to be equally important for the journey. Even when he felt tired, this thought and his father's words would fill him with a new burst of energy. There were some soldiers who would find reasons to stop on track but Yogendra was not of that kind. He conducted his task with extreme seriousness. Yogendra was of the opinion that only death could have stopped him. The seniors were often surprised by the humongous energy that the young soldiers possessed. Even though Yogendra had less experience in the field, he had made a place in everyone's heart. Yogendra strived to live up to those expectations and do something great for the nation.

The Commanding Officer soon spread out the information that the Ghatak Platoon was going to begin the attack. The soldiers for the task was not yet selected. Every soldier was in anticipation to be chosen for the mammoth mission. All companies trained to be at their best. Yogendra's porter team had been dissolved. They were training with all the other soldiers of their company, preparing for their turn. Yogendra, however, did not want to raise his hopes too high. He prayed for the stars to be on his side. One day, while Yogendra was training, he had been summoned by the Senior Officer, "How is the practice going, young man?" Yogendra stood in attention inside the officer's tent, "It is going well." The officer smiled at the young blood's enthusiasm, "I hope you are prepared. You have been selected for Ghatak." Yogendra had been waiting for this moment yet it took him by surprise, "Sir, me?" The officer nodded, "We have received recommendations from the superiors of Delta and Charlie companies. They have seen you walk continuously for 22 days on the mountain. The team wants to have such sturdy soldiers for the mission." Yogendra felt assured and confident after hearing the words of his superior.

The other Yogendra Singh also got selected for the mission. Yogendra was glad to have a familiar face in the group. They were divided into groups of five people. Lieutenant Balwan Singh Panghal was given the responsibility to lead the Ghatak Platoon. Lieutenant Balwan Singh was a newly commissioned officer who was believed to be the right choice to lead the team. After his successful venture at Tololing, he was ready to lead the soldiers to Tiger Hill. The leadership believed that the 90 degree climb required young soldiers who could complete the journey and hold on to their stamina. Ghatak Platoon was an amalgamation of soldiers from all the companies and a representative of cultural unity. The Alpha Company consisted of the Jats, the Bravo Company belonged to the Yadavs, Charlie represented the OIC, the Delta company was for the Dogras. The Ghatak Platoon did not belong to any particular caste as it was formed by soldiers from all the battalions. Four soldiers from each company were selected to form groups in the Ghatak Platoon along with a senior Havaldar, a JCO, a senior officer, and the commanding officer Balwan Singh. This made the team strong as they could all learn from each other's fighting strategies and backgrounds.

Lieutenant Balwan Singh called for a meeting with the team members, "We have been assigned a difficult task. We must rehearse the climb for a few days before we receive the instructions for the final attack." The soldiers expressed their affirmation and followed the leader's directions. Yogendra walked out of the tent hearing Singh's words floating in the air, "It is not going to be easy." Yogendra was never scared of the difficult path. He was always ready for a challenge and this time even more so as there was an aim attached to it. The soldiers were given instructions to wake up early and begin their drills of climbing the mountain. The journey till the top to Tiger was going to be much more difficult than the mock drill. The soldiers were aware of the uncertainty and wanted to be prepared for all severe situations. The drive was stronger within the soldiers as the day for the attack was right around the corner.

One morning, during their drills, Yogendra and his teammates noticed reporters around the camp. They were interviewing soldiers and officers throughout the day. The photographers were clicking pictures of the drills being performed by the soldiers. There were also videographers live streaming interviews with the Captains in charge. Singh stated in humor, "Looks like we are going to be famous."

Yogendra laughed at the remark, knowing his companions' humor well enough, "Yes, you are going to be on the front page." Their laughter had hardly died down when they noticed a young man approaching them. He had a small camera around his neck and a writing pad in his hand. He twisted the pen in his finger and fixed his glasses. All things about him highlighted that he was a reporter. Yogendra was inquisitive as to why the young man was standing before them instead of crowding around the Commander like others. The young man spoke quickly, "Sir, could I speak to you for a minute." The salutation did surprise Yogendra. He was not habituated with the term, "You wish to speak to us?" The reporter nodded, "I am interviewing soldiers from different companies to know their individual experience. I just found out that you both have been part of the porter team and have been walking for 22 days. I would really appreciate it if you could tell me something about the journey so far."

Yogendra noticed his mate taking a back step which meant he was on the spot to speak. Yogendra laughed awkwardly, "I have never given an interview before." The young man smiled in understanding, "It isn't formal, Sir. You need not be nervous. Can you tell what it felt like to walk continuously for so many days?" The reporter readied his pen and pad yet his eyes remained fixed on Yogendra. After some hesitation, Yogendra began, "It was definitely difficult but together we managed to complete all tasks." The reporter enquired, "Have you lost any of your companions or do you remember any such terrible situation that you have seen?" Yogendra felt the breath leave his lungs everytime the thought of his friend came to his mind, "I have lost my best friend Amarjeet in this war. He was an efficient and promising soldier who left too soon. Nothing can fill the void this disaster has created. We have seen the demise of many capable senior commanders. The families and the entire nation have to endure a severe loss."

The reporter could feel the immense pain in Yogendra's words, "I am so sorry for your loss. The entire nation is in debt for your services. What outcome do you see, Sir?" Yogendra smiled, "We have lost a lot.

Now it is time to win. We are going to enter the enemy camp and recapture what belongs to us. Our nation is going to be safe again. Jai Hind!" Chills ran down the young man's spine as he felt the palpable energy around him. The struggle of the soldiers and their sacrifices brought tears into his eyes. He knew he could not entirely report what he had seen and felt. Yogendra looked at his companion Singh whose glistening eyes stared back at him. Singh put his arms around Yogendra, patting his friend, "Now look who is going to be famous. Who knew you speak so well." They broke out in laughter again. Yogendra understood his friend's attempt to lighten the mood. Their only way of survival in the isolation was to not dive too deep into their emotion and for this it was important to keep themselves distracted through humor.

After the media interaction, the Commanding officer informed them that the soldiers had to gather for the 'Mandir' next day which was a holy ceremony organized to take the blessings of God before starting a mission. The soldiers had then been briefed that the mission for Tiger Hill would begin after the religious ceremony. The Platoon Havaldar addressed the soldiers, "Boys, be ready for starting the journey tomorrow. Tonight is all the time you have so, write the letters to your family. We must be prepared to face the most challenging circumstances and a farewell is due for our families." The senior did not need to say more as all soldiers were aware that worse could happen. They had all made up their minds to sacrifice their lives for the nation if circumstances demanded. Yogendra knew he may not get a chance to say the final words to his family and this letter would then remain as the final testament of his emotions. The soldiers scattered around after the meeting. Everyone is trying to process their emotions and spend time with the thoughts of their families and friends.

Yogendra had previously written letters to his family during his training at the academy and after his posting but this time it felt different. This time there was an uncertainty lurking in every soldier's mind. This might be the last medium of contact that he could establish with his family. While leaving home, Yogendra had not imagined the conditions to be so severe and now he could have only expressed himself through his letter. There were innumerable what if's floating in his mind, however, he knew none of them made any sense in that moment. Yogendra sat far from the tent, in a corner, staring at the white sheet in front of him. Yogendra let his guard down for a moment as he imagined the faces back home and began forming words on the paper. Yogendra's first letter was addressed to his parents.

July 1st, 1999
Dear Maa and Papa,

I hope this letter finds you in good health and takes away some of your worries. Papa, I know you are probably reading the letter and Maa must be standing beside you. Please tell everyone that I miss all of you. Tell Maa that I miss her the most and of course her delicious food.

I am doing well at the base and have been selected for an important task. I have been waiting for this moment for a long time. Things have not been easy as no one could have expected this massive war. It pains me to write that we have lost some of our companions including Amarjeet. I believe this war has changed all of us as people. I hope to return home soon far from the deafening sound of the artillery. The disturbing nights often make me recall your lullabies, Maa.

It is important for us to win this battle for every soul that has been lost and those that need to be saved. I need all your blessings at this hour to make my nation proud. Take all my love and give my greetings to Reena. You all always remain in my thoughts.

Your brave son,
Yogendra Singh Yadav

The letter written to his parents was easier for Yogendra as he had done that before. However, writing to Reena was completely new. The blank paper encouraged Yogendra to pour out his feelings. In very little time, Yogendra had developed a pure bond with Reena. He recollected the moments spent together and started scribbling his thoughts.

July 1st, 1999
Dear Reena,

It has been difficult for me to continue writing more often for which you must excuse me. I hope you are doing well, along with the others in the family.

It is a beautiful day as the sun shines brightly over the mountain. The radio is playing Kishor Kumar songs which you love so dearly. I imagine you are still listening to the music while going about your daily chores. Music is an important companion in our journey, often providing us the strength in times of distress. Losing dear ones has made the process even more miserable. Amarjeet's absence has kept me up throughout many nights. The recollections of the past are the only form of solace in the dark present. In this hour of crisis, I wish we had had more time to spend together. However, the moments we have enjoyed together were enough for me to know your beautiful soul. Those memories have a calming effect on my tumultuous mind. I may not have been able to fulfill all my duties as a husband as my responsibilities as a soldier demands my presence for which I apologize. I promise to return to you and spend the rest of our lives together. Your gift remains close to protect me from the dangers.

I am going for an important mission in a few hours. Pray for our victory as we need all the blessings for this mission. I hope to return to you soon. Until then take care of yourself and everyone else. You are always in my memory, keep me in yours.

Yours Loving,
Yogendra

After finishing the letter, the soldiers went about their chores. Yogendra was helping the Havaldar prepare the meal near the bonfire.

Suddenly, the wind became chilly and clouds gathered in the sky. The evening sky became darker than it had been. Before the soldiers could take shelter and move things around, a strong gust of wind hit them. Big, bold droplets hit the ground forcing people to run around trying to protect things from getting wet. Things flew around and no one could help at that moment. Yogendra pulled the cooking essentials with him but it did not help. The wind was so strong that the tents flew away along with all their essentials. The soldiers could do nothing but wait for the rain to stop. Some even wondered if this was a sign of blessing or an evil omen. Yogendra did not believe in superstitions, so he was simply annoyed. He said to Singh, "The weather is trying to mimic the enemies, making our lives difficult." Singh tried to remain positive, "Brother, this time I think it will be a blessing. Anyways, my mother used to say nature has it's own signs to bless us." Yogendra smiled at the statement. Mothers did have a way of convincing and consoling the people around them, especially their children. Yogendra believed that the world could learn a lot of positivity from mothers. It was a cloudburst which did stop within thirty minutes. However, the time was enough to get things in a mess. Soldiers stood in wet uniforms trying to collect the scattered objects on the ground.

Singh and three other soldiers picked up the tent to fix it. Meanwhile, Singh noticed, "Fellows, the letters are gone." Another soldier enquired, "What do you mean gone?" Singh kept moving blankets and clothes around, "Most of them seemed to have flown away when the wind rushed in." The soldiers looked worried at his statement. It was the last letter they were supposed to have written to their families. More soldiers came in and started looking around the area. Some letters were found near the base but most were missing. A senior officer called Yogendra, "We will fix things and put up the tent. You go and search for the letters in the bushes." Yogendra picked up his torch at the given order and walked around the camp. It was very difficult to locate small pieces of paper in the dark while the ground was still wet. Yogendra's soaked jacket did not make it any easier. He looked around and picked up as many papers as he could find. Yogendra did not read the names on the letters, so he was not aware if he did find his own letters or not. He simply collected them and brought them to the tent for the senior to read out and distribute.

Yogendra saw that the tent had been rebuilt by the time he returned. The senior took the letter and started reading out the names. Yogendra had to look for something more. He did not wait and kept looking in the tent and asking people. He had lost his wife's picture which was the only one he had with him. To his great disappointment, he could not find the picture. Turned out many people had lost their letters. Yogendra, himself found only the letter written to his parents. Singh stated, "I found only one letter. Did you find any?" Yogendra nodded, "Me too. Just one." Singh noticed Yogendra seemed low, "Don't worry. At least we have one letter. We are going to go home in no time." Yogendra smiled, "I am actually more upset about losing my wife's picture than the letter written to her." Singh suggested, "So, why don't you go out there and look again. I am sure it is there somewhere." Yogendra shook his head, "It is of no use. I did already look as much as I could in this dark. The wind has its own will. I think I am going to rely on my mind to recall her image." Singh smiled, "Isn't that the whole point of love, brother? It is beyond the material and tangible reality." Yogendra could not have agreed more or expressed his feelings in such articulate terms. Deep down that is exactly how he felt, an emotion he could not define.

On the morning of 2nd July 1999, 'Mandir' was organized. Yogendra woke up to a different morning. Not just a different day but with a feeling of some significant change. It was an important day for him as this was the first time he was going to receive the opportunity to fight in the war with his companions. It was a dream come true for Yogendra. All soldiers in the Ghatak Platoon knew that they would have to leave for the mission right after the ceremony. People were conversing among themselves, discussing the proceedings of the day. Yogendra was lost in his thoughts as he fixed his uniform. Singh called out to his mate, "You seem lost. All good?" Yogendra nodded, "I am just thinking about the mission." Singh keenly questioned, "Are you worried?" Yogendra shook his head, "No. The enemies should be worried. I am rather charged to launch the attack." There is always a need for more reassurance and encouragement on the field and Singh found strength in Yogendra's spirit. Singh nodded, "Let's go get them."

The commander in chief stood at the center chanting hymns to the lord and the soldiers circled around him, following his instruction. A unanimous voice loomed in the open space of the camp. There was a different energy in the air. Yogendra tried to connect to the universal spirit, just as the others on the ground. Yogendra's eyes focus on the floating tricolor and his heart filled with pride and warmth. His resolution became firmer with every passing moment. After the ceremony, the commander addressed the soldiers, "The soldiers of Ghatak Platoon are leaving for their mission to Tiger Hill this evening. We must all pray for their safety and victory. Soldiers, I need you to gather all the courage and give your best. The journey to the top is difficult but nothing is impossible for our soldiers. I believe in you, each one of you and so should you. Let's make our nation proud. Time to show them what we have got. Jai Hind!" Loud and enthusiastic voices joined in and repeated the mantra. Soldiers clapped and hooted to commemorate the moment and awaken the spirits with their war cry.

IX

Time for Action

On 2nd July, 1999, the Ghatak Platoon started their mission for the Tiger Hill. Camp had already been set up at the base of the hill. Soldiers were taken in vehicles till the base. They had to begin their journey to the top in the evening. Yogendra noticed synchronized movements in the soldiers assigned their tasks. Some soldiers collected their ration and ammunition. Some arranged the amenities and kept track of essentials. They had to plan for the long run, so they picked up dry fruits and biscuits which would last for longer days. The ammunition and essentials were circulated among the soldiers. They had to carry additional weight along with their personal weapons. One of the Naik's in the team carried the rocket launcher. The company also had a light machine gun, a medium machine gun and a sniper. The soldiers had to divide twenty-five magazines of bullets for the LMG among themselves. Along with a personal AK 47 and the two magazines of LMG, Yogendra was responsible to carry a five liters water tank and some ration for refreshments.

The journey started at ten in the night through the most difficult terrain. The failed attack of the 8th Battalion, Sikh Regiment in late May1999 created pressure on 182 Mountain Brigade to complete the task at all cost. Capturing the peak of the Tiger Hill was extremely important for the Indian army. It is the highest peak of the sector which provides an advantage to observe the highway connecting Srinagar to Kargil. This highway was the main supply route for the army which provided a leverage to the army that had control over the observatory point of the Tiger Hill. As the journey continued to the top, Yogendra realized that the terrain became denser and rougher. Every hundred meters felt like a thousand. The altitude made it difficult for the soldiers to breathe and continue to walk in a constant motion. Company Commander of the Charlie Company led the team, "This is just the beginning soldiers. The path is hardly half as difficult as it is going to become as we progress. We need to keep up the momentum." The constant encouragement motivated the soldiers whenever fatigue caught up to them.

The battalion kept walking throughout the entire night. They had the target to reach a location point where the 8 Sikh Regiment would already be awaiting for them. The 8 Sikh Regiment was assigned the duty of supporting the Platoon by launching an attack on the Pakistan army from the Northern and Southern end to distract the enemy. The soldiers of Ghatak Platoon managed to reach the targeted location by five in the morning. As soon as they reached, the commander informed the soldiers that they would have to take shelter behind large rocks for the time being as there could be no movement for the rest of the day. The enemy were at a vantage point for which it was easier for them to locate any movement in the daylight. The Indian soldiers needed the assistance of darkness to complete their journey. The soldiers had to spend the entire day hiding behind the rocks. Some of them were already thirsty and tired but they could not use the water they were carrying along with them. They had located a waterfall nearby which would be their saving grace. The Commander instructed, "Boys, two of you must go and bring water from the falls while the others stay on guard." Yogendra volunteered along with Singh.

Although the task was sufficient to be completed by one person, a companion was assigned to stay alert and provide backup in adverse situations. All soldiers could hear the sound of the waterfall from their way up. Yogendra and his companion did not have to walk for long before they saw the small waterfall nestled between the trees. Yogendra was mesmerized by the beauty of nature which stood in contrast to the bleakness of their situation. The crystal clear blue water was a relief to the eyes. The soldiers could not help but be spellbound by the creation of nature. The sound of the waterfall created a peaceful environment where no one could have guessed that a war was waging a few steps away. Yogendra quickly collected the water and Singh stood beside him surveying the area. They quickly went back to the troop without wasting time. The other soldiers were relieved to see them return with the water. Although they could not indulge themselves with drinking much of it, Yogendra prepared tea for everyone. Tea and biscuits became their only source of nutrition for the entire day. They had to avoid intake of water to restrict themselves from having to go to relieve themselves which would require movements. They had to be completely immobile for the entire time and lie dead behind the rocks.

On the night of 3rd July, 1999 the battalion began to climb again. The Delta Company accompanied the Ghatak Platoon. After walking for hours, the peak was clearly visible to the soldiers. Yogendra, along with the others, felt instant relief. When they reached the peak, they noticed no activity. The Delta company commander, Capt Sachin Nimbalkar stated, "I don't see enemy troops. This looks like the peak." Lt. Balwan Singh agreed, "I think we should hoist the flag on the peak." The thing about mountains is that they are unpredictable. As the soldiers took a few more steps to the top, the vision gained clarity. They realized it was not the top of the tiger hill, rather one of the peaks. Despite the disappointment, the soldiers suggested, "Sir, we should have some tea and then continue walking." The frustration was clear in Lt. Balwan's stance, "No, we shall have refreshments once we reach the top." They could see the peak from where they stood. The soldiers picked up speed and managed to cover the distance in less time. However, as they reached the next peak, they realized this was not the top either. Another snow-capped peak was waving from the distance. The soldiers were too tired and required a break. The senior officers commanded, "You may all now take some food and freshen up. We will then resume our climb."

The soldiers sat behind rocks, relaxing their tired backs for a while. Yogendra took up the responsibility to make the tea. He had just put up the stove and lit it. Suddenly, a shot came whooshing through the air towards the fire. Soldiers immediately became alert and took their stance. Lt. Balwan Singh announced, "Boys, you know what this means. We are close to the enemy. We need to be quick with our refreshments and keep moving ahead." Knowing very well that this would probably be their last meal for a long time, Yogendra quickly prepared the tea. Fear could not overpower hunger. The soldiers filled themselves with tea and biscuits. In the rough terrain and miserable condition, they were grateful for the warm drink in their hand which might as well have been their last. Meanwhile, Captain Sachin Nimbalkar had moved ahead with his team to survey the location. The Ghatak Platoon was half-way through the drink when they heard the screams of the Delta Company, "Rescue us, we are trapped." The battalion could hear and see shots being fired from the top. Movement in the daylight was risky and the Platoon could not provide support with direct fire. Lt. Balwan called the commanding officer, "Sir, Sachin and his team got stuck ahead of us. They are enduring fire from the enemy camp." The commanding officer ordered, "Instruct Sachin to lay low with his team for the time being. We will provide artillery support and rescue them once the light is out." Lt. Balwan delegated the commander's order and followed the same for his troop.

Patience is as big a part of combat as is resilience. The soldiers had to keep still for hours behind the camouflage, waiting for their time to act. Often people lose their mind under pressure situations and make rash decisions. A soldier has to be calm and alert even under the worst situations. As soon as the sky turned dark, Yogendra put out the stove. Any light could be lethal for the troop as the enemy could easily detect the light and smoke and launch fires towards their location. At around eleven in the night the Platoon decided to move at the orders of the lieutenant. They climbed a few meters ahead and located the Delta Company crouching behind boulders. They managed to pull the wounded and rescue the entire company. One of the soldiers had been hit by a bullet on their hand. Yogendra noticed another soldier clutching his face with his hand. As soon as they declined from their previous position and the soldier removed his hand, the reason became clear. The pain in his hand was so excruciating that the soldier could not control his screams. His companion quickly placed his hand back to mute the screams. They were ordered to take the wounded soldier back to base.

After hours of patience, the commanding officer finally gave out the order over radio communication, "Lt. Balwan and Captain Sachin, get your teams ready for an attack now. Ghatak Platoon will launch an attack along with some of the Delta company soldiers. Balwan and Sachin both will be leading them in the operation." Around twenty five soldiers got selected for the immediate operation, along with Yogendra. Singh and Prem were the other members from Yogendra's team who got in. Captain Sachin drew a plan map on the ground and explained the location of the enemy bunkers. All the soldiers listened to his instructions attentively. It was extremely crucial for them to be on the same page to deliver a successful plan. Captain Sachin ordered, "Both the Yogendra's will be walking as guide for the mission. So, you need to be careful and pave the path for others." While Yogendra, the young blood, saw this as an opportunity to prove himself, Singh seemed to be disappointed. Singh, his companion, was a ten year service senior to Yogendra and looked at the logistics of the situation. He objected, "Sir, why us? Our team has black cat commandos who have been a part of the Ghatak Platoon for a long time. In that case, why are we being put at risk?" It is not often that a seniors order was appreciated being questioned or challenged, however, Captain Sachin was a calm and dignified officer who tried to explain his decision, "You have been walking as porters for the entire term of the war and are familiar with the terrain. We believe you can complete this task." Until then, Yogendra was standing silently and listening to the conversation. After a point, when Singh continued to argue in a loud tone, Yogendra tried to calm him, "Let's not make so much noise. We might attract the attention of the enemies. I do now wish to get shot standing in between an argument. Singh, let us follow the order and move ahead. I am sure everything will be fine." Although Singh did not believe Yogendra's words, he somehow got convinced with a condition, "I will move ahead but you have to follow my directions which means no impulsive actions. Get it?" Yogendra accepted all terms and conditions, smiling at his companions' antiques and then they started their journey.

They quickly covered a huge distance in the dark. They had moved ahead of the rest of the company. It was very late in the night when they reached a difficult spot. Singh stopped Yogendra, "Let's wait for the rest of the team. We are too far ahead." Yogendra suggested, "Let's just try to climb a little and then we can wait at the landing." Yogendra pointed towards the space in between the mountain. Despite having some inhibitions, Singh agreed to follow, "You go first. I will climb behind you." Yogendra had no problems with the suggestion as he was eager to reach the top. Both the soldiers noticed that the ridge was steeped than before which meant they needed to be more agile. Yogendra carefully took the first few steps, accessing the geography. They took support of the rocks and pulled themselves upwards. Yogendra's tall, muscular frame was ready for such activities. Once he had covered some ground successfully, Yogendra gained more confidence. He started climbing faster and more swiftly. As he was about to reach the landing, the supporting rock holding him up dislodged out of the mountain. Yogendra's hands slipped and he rolled down the ridge. He did feel like the final moments were not very far. He groveled on the ground trying to hold on to the branches and small stones on the path, while his mind imagined the ditch waiting for his body.

Just when Yogendra was getting tired of the struggle to stop his body from rolling in a downward movement, someone clutched onto his hand. Every soldier needs a companion they can rely on. This is the reason why soldiers become each other's family. Singh was looking out for Yogendra while he climbed ahead. He acted swiftly and held on to Yogendra's hand as he watched the young soldier slipping down the ridge. Momentarily there was fear of an irreversible accident, however, it is a soldier's prerogative to be calm in such a pressure situation. One has to have strong instincts to act immediately and save his companion and Singh did just the same.

Yogendra managed to pull himself up with Singh's support, landing with only minor scratches which could have been fatal. Singh helped Yogendra fix his gear, "Remember I told you to be careful and follow instructions. You need to be a patient young man. Now you have learnt your lesson." Singh was not one to mince his words. He told the truth as it was and Yogendra appreciated his candor, although it may be a disadvantage at times. Yogendra knew his companion had good intentions at heart and would even deal with dangers for his life.

Yogendra and his companion understood that the next part of the climb could not be completed without support. They decided to hook a rope and pull themselves up on the ninety degree ridge. Singh suggested, "Let me try and hook the rope." After a couple of tries, the rope got stuck on a rock in the mountain. Singh then instructed Yogendra, "Go ahead, you should climb first." The rest of the team had appeared on the spot by then. Captain Sachin appreciated the team, "Great progress soldiers. We are right on time. Good job done by both the Yogendras." Yogendra was the first one to climb. Although the climb was comfortable for him, Yogendra took a few extra minutes to hold on to the rope and settle himself on the mountain. This time he was more careful and did not make any mistakes in a hurry. As soon as he managed to reach the landing, he helped pull the other soldiers up. Within a few minutes about seven soldiers had successfully completed the climb. The thing that they could not have predicted is that the danger was lurking right behind their neck.

The climb was not an easy one and required quite some exertion of force. Naturally such animated movements were bound to create loud noise. While the Indian soldiers were making the climb, they were completely unaware of the enemy bunkers waiting for them on both sides of the mountain. Either their movements had awakened them or they had been waiting for all soldiers to complete the climb. As soon as enough soldiers had reached the landing, the wind changed its course. Yogendra felt the first bullet move past his ears creating a buzzing effect. For a few seconds, Yogendra felt as if he had lost his hearing abilities. He had had previous gunshot encounters but never heard one so close. There was no time to contemplate on the happenings. Immediate action was necessary and all soldiers acted on impulse. The fire was so intense that the soldiers had to take cover behind the rocks. Their only advantage was the altitude at this point. They could see the enemy bunkers at a lower elevation on both sides of the ridge. After that point, no other soldier could climb the mountain, saving themselves from gunshots. The rest of the soldiers decided to remain below and observe the happenings. The one who was made through a cut of the dangling rope supporting their climb to avoid the enemies climbing from the same path which could increase the margin of risk even more.

The landing was an opening space of seven to eight meters including huge boulders. Yogendra located the enemy bunker a few feet away guarded by huge rocks and supported by distance. Two guns were clearly visible, poking out of the bunkers. The soldiers had no time to strategize. They simply had to save their lives against the sudden downpour of bullets. Without a second thought, they picked up their weapons and rained a heavy fire over the enemy bunker. The early morning fog and lowlight did provide the advantage of compromised vision. The enemy was not prepared for the intrusion at such an early hour. Their inability to spot the soldiers gave the Indian men the leverage to have a balanced fight, although initially they were taken by surprise through the open fire. They constantly lodged their bullets in the direction of the bullets for several minutes. The drowsy distracted Pakistan soldiers holding guard did not stand a chance against the eager and prepared Indian soldiers. The soldiers were able to successfully kill all the men in the bunker and capture it.

Tiger Hill top was only fifty to sixty meters above the landing where the Indian soldiers had taken refuge. Momentarily, they felt relieved to have overpowered the enemies and crossed a barrier. The soldiers had imagined completing the operation and reaching the targeted location in a few more hours. However, the sound of an attack on the lower bunker had alerted the ones above. In nature, just when individuals become comfortable, danger strikes back again. The main bunker at the peak of the Tiger Hill launched an attack on the

Indian soldiers. This was a bigger bunker than the one they had just captured. The number of soldiers in the Pakistan troop was far more than their own. Half the soldiers had not even been able to reach the landing. They not only had the advantage of height but also artillery. The Pakistan front had a buffet of ammunition including 82 motors, rocket-propelled grenade, rocket launcher, heavy machine-gun, medium machine gun, and many unidentified. The Pakistan soldiers had no intention to stop their fire. They had enough resources to keep on going for hours. They would at all costs attempt to stop the Indian's from getting to the top of the hill. There seemed to be no escape at that moment. The enemy attacked from the front and a deadly fall waited behind them. The soldiers of Ghatak Platoon were in a situation to face a large number of soldiers with advanced weapons. The odds were definitely not in their favor. Yogendra could see death rushing towards them and options of rescue appeared limited. Yet there was no fear among soldiers for losing their lives. Rather there was a deep sense of disappointment at the idea of failing their nation.

Tension filled the air and hiding behind the rocks for long started to appear impossible. The Indian soldiers were challenged by the shower of bullets launched simultaneously. The Pakistan army was relentless and showed no mercy. This enraged the India soldiers even more. Perspiration on their skin assisted the chill on their spine. They could not hear each other's voice from a close distance which was muffled by the noise of gunshots. One of the soldiers screamed, "Cowards! They can only fire shots while hiding." Another one agreed, "If only they had the guts to challenge us in combat. Then we would see who has the upper hand." The anger was justified yet it made no difference in that moment. The truth was that the enemy had an advantage and could kill them with very little effort. Yogendra's mind went back to all the deaths he had seen and the people he had lost. Their loss would only mean losing significance for the many lives that had been sacrificed in this war. Yogendra's eyes found Singh in the crowd trying to look for some assurance. Sadly his expectations were not met rather he witnessed a lot of confusion. Singh's eyes mimicked all the confusion that was coursing through all their minds. Yogendra gave himself a pep talk and tried to clear out the fog in his mind. He did not wish to die in this manner. He imagined avenging the death of his brothers. With shaking hope, Yogendra enquired, "Singh, we are going to get out of this, right?" Singh stared back at the optimistic man, "Chances are slim but we are definitely not going down without a fight. If I die today, I will take some Pakistan soldiers along with me."

X

Bite the Dust

The resolution had become firm with every passing second. The Indian soldiers had only one aim to kill as many opponents as possible before death engulfs them. The Platoon Havaldar, Madan observed, "There is no way for us to return now. We have to get inside the enemy bunkers." Yogendra was aware of similar situations which did not turn out well, "Sir, they might have planted mines near the bunker. There would be nothing left of our body if we encountered one." Yogendra had seen fellow soldiers dying from such mine attacks in the past during his mission to eradicate terrorist activities in Srinagar. He had also heard officers fighting in the Tololing war speaking about Pakistan's strategy. When the rescue team went to extract the dead bodies of the soldiers, they would have to meet their own death due to the previously planted bombs and grenades on the bodies. They would put multiple such traps near their bunkers and dead bodies which would instantly take out multiple soldiers approaching the area at a time. The other soldiers were also worried about the consequence of Yogendra's statement turning out to be true. They would be dead before being able to fight the opponents which was not the preferable conclusion under any circumstance.

The Platoon Havaldar's loud voice loomed next, "Men, if we don't move, we are dying from bullets. So, I would rather take my chance with the mines and try my best to save myself. Let us first safeguard ourselves from the enemy that we can see and then we can think of the invisible one. Rab Rakha." The soldiers immediately felt energized from his words. Thirst for life was so strong that the soldiers transcended the ten meters distance within a flash. They crawled with all the power within themselves. Yogendra could feel the air dry out of his lungs, yet he did not stop to contemplate. He could not waste even a second to catch his breath. The enemy was ready to take the opportunity to end their lives. The Indian soldiers jumped inside the enemy bunker and began pulling the dead bodies out. There was still the looming risk of the dead bodies having grenades attached to them. However, they had no time for fear as the intensity of the fire from the top bunker had increased. Their only shelter to protect themselves was the enemy bunker.

Just like his companions, Yogendra held onto the leg of one of the bodies and dragged it out of the bunker. As he was pulling the dead body of the Pakistan soldier, Yogendra's eyes landed on his face. Strangely it did not look any different. He did not know what he had expected to see on an enemy's face but he had not expected such familiarity. The man lying dead at his foot was like any other ordinary man in his twenties. Yogendra had never had such a close encounter with the enemy and he had not had the opportunity to look at their faces. Despite such familiarity, Yogendra did not understand the reason behind such hatred which could lead to war. So many young lives had been lost for reasons which did not make any sense at that moment. No agenda or politics seemed to be substantial in front of lives lost. Yogendra, however, knew that his nation had put in all efforts to stop the massacre and fight for the peace that matters. In that moment, Yogendra was simply proud to represent the motherland that has truly treated it's children like a nurturer, not willing to destruct rather striving to protect and secure.

The Indian soldiers began fixing the bunker according to their need. They blocked the side facing the top bunker and opened the one which faced the path they had taken. They could see the top bunker at the peak and so could the Pakistan army sitting on top. The India soldiers gained more confidence after taking guard. At the orders of the Platoon Havaldar, the soldiers opened fire. Both the opponents continued to fire shots continuously for five hours. The

PlatoonHavaldar was a man of short stature and high spirits. He would take a jump over the rocks and draw out the entire magazine of bullets. Yogendra and the Havaldar were the only ones carrying AK47s. Rest of the team had snipers and other ammunition. Yogendra became worried by the impulsive action, "Sir, we do not have enough ammunition. If you keep shooting in this manner, we will be left with nothing." The Havaldar noticed his bullets were almost over, "You lend me some for now." The soldiers were always there to support each other but having no ammunition would be of no help to anyone. Yogendra was hesitant as he himself had limited stock. He knew once the bullets are over, neither will he be able to protect himself nor anyone else.

Yogendra informed the Havaldar, "I do not have much with me. I can only lend you one magazine. After this you are on your own." The other soldiers in the team also started getting worried. As time went by their inventory kept decreasing. Without ammunition the war would be lost in no time. They decided to ask for help from the ones who could not climb up the ridge. Yogendra screamed out, "Our stock is low. We need ammunition. Throw it upwards." The soldiers tied the bullets and magazines in a handkerchief and threw it over the ridge. It managed to fall on the landing, however, it was far from the bunker. To get hold of the ammunition, Indian soldiers would have to risk getting out of their bunker and pick up the resource. The weather was bright and sunny which did not support their objective. As the vision was clear, the enemies easily located the bundle of bullets and magazines on the ground. It only took a minute for the Pakistan soldiers to rain shots over the buddle. The shot did not stop as if challenging the Indians to approach the ammunition. Yogendra and his companions knew well that anyone who approached the bundle would be shot directly on their head and there would be no chance to be alive.

They decided to save their lives and let the ammunition remain on the ground. None of the soldiers approached the article which had by then been broken and scattered by the beating of the gunshots. Very few bullets remained to support the soldiers. Yogendra suggested, "This is my last magazine and I sure the others are on the edge as well. We must stop the fire." The PlatoonHavaldar reasoned, "But the fire was keeping the enemies away. They will start approaching if we stop the fire." Yogendra nodded, "I agree with you, Sir but without the bullets, our guns are just sticks. We are not able to see the enemy from this distance, therefore, none of the shots would hit the target." We would be completely ineffective. At least with our ammunition we have a chance to fight if the opponents approach." When the men noticed this rapid decline of ammunition, they agreed with Yogendra and decided to save the rest. The Platoon Havaldar commanded, "Alright, soldiers, hold your fire and lay low." Now began the real game of patience. Until now, the enemies which were at about fifty meters distance could easily hear them. They had to change their stance and remain completely silent. Yogendra believed that it was harder to wait than to attack. The constant urge to check the approaching enemies was difficult to control. He kept his mind at peace and so did the others. All that remained was to wait for the opponent's move.

The fire had stopped for quite some time after the Pakistan army motors had launched a heavy attack. About twenty minutes had passed which only indicated to the Pakistan army that either the Indian soldiers were dead or their ammunition had expired. In either case, the Pakistan army believed to have the upper hand in that situation. They had to come and check the situation at the landing. The superior ordered about twenty five soldiers to climb down to the bunker and confirm the happenings. The Indian soldiers were holding their breath. The approaching opponents were clearly audible. There were soft conversations and commands being passed among them. The Indian soldiers had taken refuge behind three massive rocks in groups of two and three. Yogendra felt the cold sweat tickle down his forehead. The look of uncertainty was evident on each one's face. This could be the game changer and give them the confidence they so dearly needed. Overtaking the Pakistan soldiers would also rattle the ones in the bunker above. However, their strength was low compared to the number of opponents. Adding to that the ammunition was limited which had to be strategically used. Their only solution would be close combat which could be rewarded by the decreasing distance. The sound of the steps kept getting louder with every passing second. Yogendra closed his eyes praying to God and preparing for the showdown.

The Indian soldiers pretended to be dead and waited for the enemy soldiers to come closer. They had already coordinated the plan among themselves. The Pakistan soldiers approached, carefully surveying the area. The bodies of the Indian soldiers were still not visible to them. They had to move closer to the bunker. It was only a matter of time when the opponents reached near the shooting range. Yogendra watched the men loosely holding on to their AK47s. He then looked at Singh sitting beside him who simply nodded to give a go ahead. There was complete silence in the Indian camp. They did not need words to communicate instructions of charge. Platoon Havaldar, Madan raised his thumb to give the final order. The Indian soldiers did not allow the enemies any time to think and open fire on them in unison. The Pakistan soldiers were taken by surprise. Before they could steady their weapons and pull the trigger, the rush of bullets had washed them away. Most of the men were dead within seconds and the rest did not take any chance to fight back. Two soldiers escaped to save their lives. Once they reached their bunker, they informed their commanding officer about the Indian soldiers being alive.

The location of the Indian troop had become more accurately known to the Pakistan army. After the attack on the Pakistan soldier, their strength had also been detected. The two soldiers who escaped from the landing had estimated that there were about ten soldiers in the Indian troop which was then delegated to the commanding officers. In this situation, this knowledge was power for the Pakistan army and made the position of Indian soldiers more vulnerable. The upside of this situation for the Indian soldiers was finding more ammunition. They picked up the weapons stranded by the dead

Pakistan soldiers. More AK47s and snipers were added to their resources. Madan instructed, "Search their bodies, you may find bullets and magazines." Yogendra did as was instructed. He crawled and pulled one of the bodies. They had to be careful not to touch any grenades if at all planted. The dead soldier had been shot on his chest. Blood was still oozing out of the newly created whole. His face was marred by the dirt and dust on the ground. Yogendra searched his pockets and found a few magazines in the right one. When Yogendra put his hand in the left pocket, he found a purse. Without spending much time, Yogendra pushed the findings in his pocket and crawled back and took shelter behind the rock.

Yogendra sat down and looked at the wallet in his hand which consisted of nothing but a photograph of a woman. The photograph was covered in dirt. Yogendra rubbed it against his shirt to be able to see it properly. The woman appeared to be in her twenties draped in saree. Yogendra instantly assumed it to be the dead soldier's wife. His mind took him to the thoughts of his own wife. Yogendra could not imagine the pain that would be inflicted on the woman by the news of his dead husband. It had suddenly hit him, the majestic effect of the consequences of this war. The broken families and the bereaved relatives. He threw the empty wallet to the side. Yogendra was not sure why but he kept the photograph along with him. This would probably remind him of the lives being lost. Also it filled him with motivation to return home to his wife who must be waiting as eagerly to see him.

In the meantime, Yogendra also spotted the difference between the Indian soldiers and the Pakistan soldiers. While the Indian men fight till the last drop of blood in their body, the opponents decide to run. An Indian soldier would never leave behind his companion to die. Yogendra, himself, would give all his efforts to save the life of his companion. The Pakistan soldiers were far more strategic in their approach. They would rather save their lives in the moment and plan a counter attack in the future. This is the reason the last two men did not stay back to defend their brother. They went back to provide information to their superiors who would then act accordingly on their behalf. The bodies of their companions lying behind did not matter at that moment. All they focused on was to win the war. The opponents did not fight with the same amount of emotions as the Indian troops. For the Indian soldiers, the life of their companions was as important as winning the war. Yogendra believed that a country is nothing without it's people. Therefore, it is important to save all lives that will make the country glorious.

After about twenty five minutes of no activity, danger was knocking back at the Indian front. As soon as the two soldiers had delivered the news regarding the Indian soldiers, the commanding officers of the Pakistan army began strategizing. As the Indian soldiers were lesser in strength, the Pakistan officers decided to send about thirty five soldiers to wipe out the entire Indian troop. The Pakistan soldiers were certain that this would discourage future attacks instantly. Thirty five Pakistan soldiers began moving downwards towards the bunker on the landing. As soon as the movement began, the Pakistan army in the top bunker started providing cover fire to their companions. Constant firing for several minutes alerted the Indian soldiers regarding the attack. Yogendra and his companions were certain that it was a cover fire and the enemy was approaching soon. The Indian soldiers coordinated among themselves. The Platoon Havaldar, Madan instructed, "Soldiers, each of you take guard behind single rocks. Prem you will be handling the rocket launcher, so you must stay ahead. Rest follow each other's lead and take your time and aim at the target." The Indian soldiers were not in a rush. They were again going to wait for the opponents to go close to the shooting range. However, this time they were more confident as they had all the ammunition support. All they needed to do was have patience and aim at the targets accurately.

The Pakistan soldiers were easily detectable as they ascended through the only possible pathway, however, they were protected by their cover fire. The enemy troops in the top bunker used all the ammunition they possessed including grenades, rocket launchers, machine guns and AK47s. Yogendra watched the steady steps getting closer to their hideout. Prem, one of his team members, was sitting behind the rock adjacent to him with the rocket launcher placed in front of him. His hand was lying calmly on the trigger. Feeling eyes staring back at him, Prem looked back at Yogendra. They exchanged a look of assurance and that was all the encouragement they could muster from each other in that moment. As the Pakistan soldiers came closer, they instantly spotted the barrel of the rocket launcher hoisted on a rock. They did not take any time to charge. All their rocket-propelled grenades were targeted towards the barrel of the rocket launcher. The barrel could not sustain the attack for long and was completely damaged. The impact of the firing was so strong that the rocks went flying in the air and hit Prem on his face. He could not remain seated behind the rocket launcher as it was being heavily targeted. Prem left his spot and went running towards the Platoon Havaldar.

Yogendra watched Prem taking guard near the Platoon Havaldar. Right then Yogendra heard Madan scream, "Yogendra, throw the LMG towards me." Yogendra knew that the light machine gun was the only weapon with them that could resist the heavy fire of the Pakistan troops. He quickly picked up the weapon and threw it towards the Havaldar. No sooner had he thrown the object than the scenario completely changed. Yogendra's eyes landed on the rocks above them. Ten Pakistan soldiers were standing on top of them, ready to fire in no time. Yogendra could feel the lump at the back of his throat. He did not think there could be any path to escape. Yogendra called out to Madan, "Sir, the soldiers are standing right on top." Madan vision was barred by the rocks, "How many?" By the time Yogendra could answer the question the Pakistan soldiers had heard their voices. It was not impossible to do so as they were only ten meters away. As soon as Yogendra's location became clear to the opponents, they immediately threw a grenade at him.

The artillery landed in between Yogendra and his companion. Singh had taken guard beside Yogendra. He was firing from behind, providing cover to the ones in front. Before they could comprehend what had happened, the grenade that had landed between them burst. The impact rattled the soldiers. They were disheveled from their positions behind the rock. Yogendra felt the world become completely deaf. This was hundred times more intense than the numbing feeling of the whooshing bullet. Yogendra watched things move in slow motion as he attempted to orient himself. His disoriented mind could hardly process the situation. Yogendra picked himself up, ready to defend himself. He shook his head and jerked his shoulders, patting the dirt of his face and body. Parts of his uniform were tattered and his wife's locket was torn. Yogendra noticed the locket lying beside him. The heavy impact and movement of his large frame may have resulted in the locket getting torn from his neck. The locket immediately reminded him of the things waiting for him back at home. He picked up the small locket and put it inside his shirt's pocket. Yogendra understood that it was his destiny to be alive which meant he had more opportunity to fight back.

Yogendra was brought back by the sound of Singh's voice, "Yogendra, I think I just lost my hand." Yogendra was taken aback by the statement. He quickly turned to look at his companion. Singh was behind a rock a few steps behind Yogendra. He noticed that Singh was still holding on to his gun. Yogendra was relieved to notice that Singh had not lost his hand but rather a finger. The grenade had chopped off Singh's right hand index finger. The pain was so intense that Singh assumed to have lost his hand. Yogendra assured, "Brother, it is not your hand. You have lost your finger." Yogendra crawled near his companion's rock. Singh shares the relief as it was much better news than losing his hand. Yogendra watched blood gushing out of the wound. However, the man in front of him appeared to be made out of steel. Singh made no sounds of complaint. Yogendra enquired, "Where is your field dressing? We need to stop the bleeding." Singh shook his head, "I don't have it." Yogendra assured, "Wait, I have mine. This will do for now. Let me tie this together." Yogendra swiftly tied the bandage over the wound, stopping the heavy flow of blood.

On the other hand, Prems' wounds were worse than they had appeared. The Indian soldiers were struggling to keep up a brave front. The continuous fire did not and in between that they had to nurture their wounds. Yogendra advised Singh, "You should jump down. Both you and Prem are wounded and need to be treated. You will not be able to fire without your active hand." Although it was a twenty feet jump, Yogendra thought that it was a better option. Staying in that place meant definite death to Yogendra. He thought that jumping down would give the wounded soldiers a better chance at survival. Singh did not agree, "No, I am not going anywhere. We can help reload the weapons and assist with other ammunition. The team needs us here as our strength is already low." Yogendra was not really satisfied by the decision as he wanted his companions to be safe. However, he understood Singh's emotions as he himself would have done the same.

Yogendra had only read about soldiers' sacrifices in books. Now he himself had witnessed the selfless love of a soldier for his country and companions. Singh was ready to sacrifice his life and risk everything he had back at home. He could have saved himself by leaving the space but he decided to stay and help fellow soldiers. Singh wanted to fight for his nation with his companions until his last breath. He did not want to run away from the situation like the Pakistani soldiers. There was no condition in the love portrayed by a soldier. Singh had proved the purity of such emotions for Yogendra. In reality, this was Yogendra's first experience of such sacrifice. He was a young soldier in the army who had no prior experience. Yogendra was overwhelmed by the display of such emotions which were once only imaginary. He felt proud to be under the tutelage of such seniors who were constantly teaching him new lessons. They were fighting for each other without thinking about their own lives. This was the strength of the Indian army.

XI

String of Hope

In life, there are some moments that completely wash out of people's mind but there are some where every second remains etched in a person's mind. Yogendra was experiencing one such moment where every breath felt thousand years long. Yet Yogendra himself was not aware how clearly he would remember every second of this experience in his future. Yogendra was almost done tending to Singh when he hear Madan's voice, "We need cover here." Once the Pakistan army had disabled the rocket launcher and the light machine gun, they shifted their focus on the sniper. The sniper was positioned beside the Platoon Havaldar. They targeted the sniper and threw continuous shots at him. From three directions bullets were launched at him. Yogendra's roommate Grenadier Anantram instructed him, "You should go and help out the sniper." Yogendra followed the seniors order without any questions. He waited for the right time to move to be able to dodge the bullets.

Yogendra noticed that the Pakistan soldiers were completely focused on the sniper. He warranted it to be the accurate moment to run towards the Platoon Havaldar's hideout. It was not long before the enemy spotted movement on the ground. Their vision was their power at that moment. They could clearly see each step taken by the Indian army from the elevated view point. Yogendra ran quickly but it was not fast enough to avoid the enemy's attack. As the Pakistan soldiers noticed Yogendra running, they threw another grenade directed towards Yogendra. Luck was not in Yogendra's favor as a grenade splinter hit Yogendra's leg. He instantly dropped to the ground and his first thought was that he has lost his foot. Yogendra tapped his leg with his hand to check if his foot was intact. He was grateful to have his foot in place. However, there was a deep cut wound on his leg and blood flew out heavily. Yogendra needed to stop the blood flow. He had already lent his strip to Singh, so he needed another way to manage his wound. He felt excruciating pain starting from his knee till his foot. Yogendra had a black bandana around his neck. He pulled the bandana out with his left hand and hit it with a piece of rock. The bandana was shortened and Yogendra attempted to tie it around his neck.

Yogendra was distracted tying his wound when another grenade came flying through the air. There was no time to react. A splinter from the grenade hit Yogendra's nose. The impact created a long gash that began above his nose and stretched till the portion below his right eyes. Yogendra dropped to the ground and held on to his nose. The world for him was moving in spirals. He had never felt such pain and dizziness all at once. His hands on his nose assured him that it was in place, however, his wet shirt was worrisome. The uniform had become darker as blood seeped into it. After a few minutes, Yogendra opened his eyes but he could not see anything. His mind imagined the worst possible conclusion which was his vision being impaired. Yogendra thought to himself that nothing could have been worse than losing his eyes. A slight panic did hit him as there was nothing he could have done without his vision. Yogendra's entire face had become numb and he did not think he could be much productive at that moment.

Yogendra could hear the voice of his Platoon Havaldar Madan which meant that he had come closer to his side. He still could not see anything, so he screamed, "Sir, I am not able to see anything. I think I have lost both my eyes." Havaldar Madan enquired, "Are you sure there is not even partial vision?" Yogendra replied, "No, Sir. My face is completely numb and there is a deep wound over my nose. I think a splinter from the grenade has hit me." Yogendra could not express his pain through screams. He has never been one to emote freely. He lay on the ground silently absorbing his pain. Yogendra slowly opened his eyes with time. He saw blood droplets dripping down his nose on the ground below. This time a look at his shirt told him that he had lost a lost of blood. He was not sure what he could do to stop this wound. Yogendra's eyes fell on a white sleeping bag which belonged to the Pakistan soldiers. He picked it up and held over his open wound. Yogendra's hand kept wiping the blood with the bag. The blood, however, did not stop even after several attempts. Yogendra's hands and face were painted with blood.

Yogendra understood he needed help and decided to pull himself towards the sniper. He crawled with a lot of effort to reach the corner. Once he reached near the sniper, Yogendra supported his back against the wall. The sniper, Tarun, was sitting right in front of him behind a boulder. His senior, Grenadier Anantram was sitting on his left, with his back towards the wall as well. Seeing Yogendra in distress, Anantram had decided to move ahead and help Tarun. Yogendra was wiping the blood off his face when Tarun noticed, "You have a bad wound there brother." Yogendra nodded, "I need your help to treat this. Too much blood has already been lost." Tarun replied, "Hold on for a while. I won't be able to move right now. Keep firing for a little while. I will be there with you some time." Yogendra could not feel any pain. His face and leg were completely numb. He picked up the gun with his right hand and kept firing. The blood dripping down his face was an intrusion. He used his other arm to rub the blood off his face.

Yogendra was trying to muster up all the energy to keep on firing. In the meantime, Tarun found space to tend to his wound, "Let's do this quick. You keep on providing cover fire." Tarun shifted his eyes from the enemy and fished out the field strip. He had put the packet near his mouth to tear the covering of the strip. Suddenly, Yogendra watched Tarun's body drop to the ground. The field strip still tightly clutched in his hand, now lay on the soil. Yogendra looked at his face and noticed the small hole on his forehead. Tarun had been shot straight on his head right when he looked away from the opponent. Yogendra could not believe his eyes. Here was this man minutes before, trying to help him and now he was a lifeless corpse. Yogendra could not help but it was because of him that Tarun was distracted and faced the consequences. Yogendra knew there was no logical conclusion behind his thoughts as danger and death were the most certain outcomes in the war. He watched the young face of the sniper and his mind filled with rage. Yogendra could not accept such honourable men losing everything in a matter of minutes.

Yogendra pulled Tarun's hand but there was no activity in his body. He then opened Tarun's clenched fist and took out the packet of field strips. He still needed help to tend to his wound. Yogendra turned to his left to call out to Anantram who was sitting a little distance from him. He informed, "Anantram, Tarun is dead. He got shot in the head." There was shock in Anantram's eyes, "What?" This was the only word that came out of Anantram's mouth before he fell on Yogendra's lap. Anantram's body was limp. Yogendra could not fathom what had just happened. He looked at the man lying on his lap in astonishment. There was a bullet injury on his chest. Yogendra pressed his hand on the wound and shook the man, "Anantram, can you hear me?" Sadly, he was far gone and could hear nothing. Yogendra knew this well enough but watching his companions fall was extremely painful.

As soon as the Pakistan army understood that they had leverage over the decreasing number of Indian soldiers, they moved closer. The enemy jumped down from the mountain onto the landing, covering the area from both sides. The Indian army did not have any other protection but the rocks while the advantage of distance was completely washed. The opponents started to launch heavy fire on the Indian soldiers. Yogendra and his companions had nothing to do but fire back. Their large number was an advantage which the Indians could not overcome. Shots were fired from both sides and lives were lost. Yogendra kept firing until fatigue caught up to him. His eyes became heavy and vision was blurred. It may have also been difficult to keep eyes open due to the dust and particles enveloping them from the action of the artillery. Yogendra had no information about his companions. All of them remained scattered throughout the attack. Yogendra had only one resolution that he had to kill as many Pakistan soldiers as possible. Until his body surrendered, Yogendra was not going to remove his fingers from the trigger. The noise of the gunshots and the hazy vision had transported Yogendra into a trance. The numbness in his body had traveled to his mind and memories flashed in front of his eyes.

Yogendra's mind took him back to his training days at the academy. The drills had appeared to be the most difficult thing for the cadets in the academy. Back then Yogendra did not know what awaited him in the future. The drills were merely preparing them for the real deal. On some days the cadets were taken through mock missions. These missions were constructed like real life scenarios. One such day was recalled into Yogendra's mind. The cadets stood on the field prepared to work out the drills like every day. Yogendra had started training with his peer a few months back. He was still mesmerized to be in the presence of the soldiers and officers, doing what he had desired. One of the Ustaad addressed the batch, "You will be divided in groups today which will be your Platoon. Direction will be provided to play out a mock attack scenario. Your seniors will participate as the opponents attacking your territory which you will have to protect and recapture. Understood?" All the cadets loudly proclaimed their affirmation. Everyone was excited to learn and experience something new, not knowing what waited for them.

The cadets were placed in a war-like situation. The entire operation was planned inside the woods surrounding the camp. Cadets were placed in five groups. Yogendra was placed in Platoon B, along with Amarjeet and eight other soldiers. They had no food that morning and were only provided one bottle of water for the rest of the day. A huge bag of weights was put on their shoulders to make it even more difficult. The other thing they had was a rough map of the area informing them about the location of the enemy. Their task was to surround the enemy territory and capture it through strategy and hand to hand combat. They also had to rescue a mannequin captives on their mission. During the exercise, the soldiers would be introduced to equipment for surveillance, tracking and identification of the enemy. The soldiers would be required to sense and neutralize mock IEDs and mines. Once the member of the team had been pinned by the enemy, they would be regarded as eliminated. The team that was able to locate the enemy base, capture it, save the hostage and hoist their team flag first would be deemed as the winner of the drill.

The entire drill was scattered around a huge area that the cadets had to cover on foot. Yogendra's team chose him as the leader who would strategize and give instructions. Yogendra divided different tasks and divided them into teams of three and four. Being divided helped them to survey the area easily. Yogendra, Amarjeet and Sunil moved towards the assigned direction. It was not easy walking with ten kilograms of weight on their back in the month of May. They had just begun walking and their entire uniform was soaked. Parched lips and dry throats begged for water but they had to be very careful to use the little stock that they had with them. There were several huddles on the way that they had to be careful about. Yogendra and his companions were midway when he noticed something different. The grass on the ground seemed different in front of them. Yogendra commanded, "Stop! There might be mines. Look the grass has a different color. We need to check." Yogendra dropped to the ground and slowly removed the heap of grass and leaves. Turned out he was correct the path was blocked by a string of IEDs that were interconnected.

They knew these were not real yet they were scared to fail the test which would result in some or the other punishment. They had been given a demo in class to deactivate the device but never had they performed such in a practical situation. Three of them looked at each other trying to encourage the other to take the first step. Amarjeet observed, "Yogendra, you should do it. Your hands are steady." Yogendra was not one to run away from a challenging situation. He stated, "Alright, I will do it but you should know I cannot give any guarantees to nail this." Everyone was on the same boat, so it was a fair bet. Yogendra discussed with the other three all through the process. Stopping and racking their heads to remember the next step. This seemed to be a more advance device which was virtually controlled. None of them had any hopes about cracking it but luck favored them. They managed to cut the right wires and the automated device indicated the successful diffusion.

They had taken two steps when three men jumped on them from the trees. They were taken by surprise yet acted on instinct. Yogendra, immediately, swung his arm to defend himself and so did the others. Amatjeet used the heavy bag to push the opponent to the ground. All three of them successfully pinned the enemy and moved ahead. Coming across the enemy only meant they were close to the destination. The ten people in their group coordinated through whistles. Some of them had been taken down by the seniors. Yogendra met some people of his team almost close to the enemy camp. He noticed one of them sitting by the tree while the others tended to him. Yogendra enquired, "What happened?" The other cadet replied, "I think it is a heat stroke." Yogendra quickly offered the water to them, "I think we are close to the base. This would be the right time to use the water. Let him rest here. We should move on ahead." They had started in the morning and the daylight was on the verge of disappearing. The entire day they had to face different tasks along the way and face combat with the opponents. This was the final bout that was waiting for them.

They noticed at a corner there was a half broken shed. Yogendra knew this had to be it. They boys smiled at each other to have finally found the destination. They had to pin down multiple opponents on the way. Their backs had almost given up by the weight and there was very little energy left to carry. They had scratches all over their body and simply wanted to end the mission and return to the camp. Amarjeet rushed in, "Let's get this over with." He entered the shed first and turned to another room at the back. Amarjeet took long swift steps to enter the room. Right when Yogendra pulled at his shirt and he fell backwards. Amarjeet looked in shock, "What the hell? Why did you do that?" Yogendra did not say a word and simply looked at the bottom of the door frame. Amarjeet and the others noticed a white string attached to both sides of the frame. Sunil opined, "Woh! We had almost lost it. Good catch, Yogendra." The cadets then took careful steps around the shed, avoiding any more mishaps. After looking around the entire space. They finally found the mannequins locked by a multi-level lock which they had to crack. They unlocked the mannequin after some trials and hoisted the flag on a market portal. The green signal on the indicator marked the successful completion of their drill. Amarjeet jumped and hugged Yogendra. This was their first victory together.

Yogendra's eyes opened as he felt the warmth of Amarjeet's embrace and the happiness of the victory. Dust and dirt still disturbed his vision but he was out of the trance, taking in the surroundings. Yogendra did not know why his mind took him back to the memory of this day. His friend had passed away then why did it all feel so real. As if he could hear the sound of Amarjeet's joyous laughter. Probably he needed to feel his lost friend's presence or the young indomitable spirit of his companions cherishing the minor success as if they had won the world. Whatever it may have been, Yogendra realized he was filled with a new found energy and zeal. He was suddenly more attuned to the surroundings. As his vision slowly cleared, he watched several footsteps walking around the space in front of him. Their uniforms indicated they were Pakistan soldiers. The men kept moving closer and their forms began to appear like giants. Yogendra's limp form was still supported by rocks. There were about twenty of them. Yogendra had no clue about his companions but considering the heavy fire, logic would say that they were dead. However, it was strange that he had not been hit by a single bullet during the attack. After all this, Yogendra somewhere still had hope and that is the only thing one could have while looking death in the eyes.

XII

Till the Last Drop

1300 hours, 4th July 1999

The Pakistan army continuously attacked the Indian soldiers for an hour. The Indian soldiers defended themselves with heavy counter fire. Yogendra could not remember when the firing had stopped from their end. When his trance was broken, he noticed the Pakistan army standing a few feet away. The commanding officer of the Pakistan troop ordered, "Soldiers, go and check if any of them is alive." Yogendra knew what this meant. He had never experienced it but he had learnt it during training. The way to check if the enemy is alive would be to shoot them again. The commanding officer continued, "We must clear out the area quickly. This has been going on for too long. Questions are now being asked from the high command." The soldiers nodded and scattered around the landing. Indian soldiers were all settled behind separate rocks. Yogendra watched with open eyes as tall men in pathani suits started walking towards his companion. Yogendra's body remained still, supported by the rock while his eyes took in the information.

The Pakistan soldiers began from the farthest end. Yogendra could not see them but could hear their movements. There was some scratching sounds along with some mumble. After which came the sound of three gunshots. Yogendra knew that the Pakistan men were shooting at the bodies of his companions. His body burned in rage as he could do nothing but watch. Anger could land him dead in the moment. He had to keep his cool and defend himself. After several shots, Yogendra watched the men walk towards Officer Tarun.

Yogendra had watched Tarun being shot on the head. Tarun was lying directly in front of Yogendra. The Pakistan soldiers approached the body and kicked it with their foot. Then without a second of thought, plunged three shots on it. The immobile body jumped a few feet from the ground from the impact of the shots. Yogendra felt the sound of the bullets were almost deafening in the deadly silence. Some parts of the bodies got detached and thrown in different directions.

Yogendra remained still as the Pakistan soldier walked towards him. His eyes were opened but the body mimicked a dead one. The enemy had come to check if he was dead and he had to convince them. The Pakistan soldier had his face covered with a black scarf. However, his stature and voice was that of a man in early twenties. He could have very well been of the same age as Yogendra. The opponent screamed out, indicating to Yogendra, "Here is another one. His eyes are open but looks to be dead." Another man replied, "Come on, be done with him now. We need to be sure." The young soldier picked up his weapon and shot Yogendra on his left upper arm. Yogendra could see, from his peripheral vision, the smoke being released from his burned shirt caused by the bullet. The warm blood seeping out of Yogendra's arms stood in contrast with the cold surrounding him. Yogendra did not let any sound leave his lips. He remained as animated as the dead. Yogendra knew that to be alive this was his only possible way out.

Yogendra was recovering from the first shot on his upper arm, when the soldier fired two consecutive shots on both his thighs. By now, blood was flowing out of my body like a river. Yogendra could feel his pants getting completely drenched. The rough land forms and rapid movements had left very little of the uniform worn by him. The torn and tattered cloth had lost all abilities to provide Yogendra any warmth. A strong chill ran down Yogendra's spine. He could not afford to shiver in the cold or cry out in pain. Yogendra had a lot of tolerance for pain, however, nothing prepared him for that moment. The soldier's eyes were fixed on him. A few minutes appeared to be yearlong. Even the slightest movement could be lethal. Although

Yogendra was in intense pain, he calmed his mind and controlled his breathing. The silence was so deep that slight changes in breathing could be spotted. More than bodily strength, Yogendra knew that only the power of his mind could save him.

After a few seconds, the Pakistan soldier could not spot any activity and moved away from Yogendra. All the Pakistan men were convinced that the Indian soldiers were dead. They shot on all the bodies and none showed any sign of life. The soldiers went and informed their company commander, standing a few meters away. The officer screamed, "Well done boys! We needed to clear the space and we have successfully achieved it. The stupid Indian army thought we would let them take over Tiger Hill. It is not in their capacity to overpower us. We are going to kill each one of them and win this war." Yogendra could hear every word. His skin crawled to hear such animosity in the enemy's voice. The man went about cursing and abusing the India army for a long time. His subordinates joined in with laughter and agreements. There was arrogance in their tone but also relief to have secured a major position in the war.

Meanwhile the Delta Company at the Mushkoh were hitting the Pakistan camp at the Tiger Hill top with medium machine guns. The Pakistan ordered, "We have to capture Mushkoh valley and uproot the Indian soldiers. If the fire continues to build, it will create more nuisance for us. We are going to attack the Mushkoh valley with a plan. Yogendra quietly heard the conversation and became worried. If the Pakistan army attacked on the Delta Company, the Indian soldiers from Mushkoh will be ready to plunge a counter attack on them. The problem in this situation will be faced by the Indian soldiers trying to get to the Tiger Hill top. These soldiers will get stuck in between the attack of the two camps. Yogendra did not want this for his companions as it would only result in death. The Indian soldiers will lose any path to escape. Yogendra could only pray at that moment to remain alive so that he could deliver the news to his seniors. Receiving the prior information of the attack could be highly beneficial for the Indian army to protect themselves.

The radio set that the Platoon Havaldar had was broken by the Pakistan soldiers. The only way to transfer the news would be for Yogendra to reach his people, who seemed to be extremely far away at that moment. Yogendra grit his teeth and swallowed his pain. He kept his patience and waited for the Pakistan army to leave. Yogendra was looking for an opportunity to escape. The Pakistan soldiers walked around the landing translating information and orders through their radio connection. Some men were talking ill about the Indian army and cursing the dead on the ground. After a while, the Pakistan Commanding officer instructed the soldiers, "Pick up all the weapons belonging to the Indian soldiers. We have to get back to the camp and prepare for the attack on Mushkoh." Two soldiers went on a second round. One of them picked up the weapons on the ground, while the other shot the dead Indian soldiers again. This was also a medium for the Pakistan soldiers to display their rage. Yogendra was still alive and not among the dead. Just when he had thought about his escape, uncertainty regarding death returned.

The two men came close to him. One of them picked up the AK47 that was lying near his hand. The other soldier fired two shots at this arm and leg. Yogendra remained silent. His resilience could not be broken. In his mind, Yogendra was so determined that he believed he would survive if the Pakistan soldier did not shoot him in the head or heart. He used that belief positively to charge himself and keep the hope alive. Once the soldier had picked up his weapon and checked the area, both of them began moving. Yogendra's resolution became stronger. Despite the amount of injuries, he had the hope and desire to live. He could see more chances of himself escaping from the place. However, the optimism was short-lived. The young Pakistan soldier took a few steps away from Yogendra and turned back to look at him. Yongendra had no idea what were his reasons for stopping mid-way, until he raised his gun at Yogendra. The Pakistan soldier aimed at Yogebdra's heart. Although there was no sign of life, the soldier wanted to be completely thorough with his check.

Yogendra's chance at life became flimsier as the soldier steadied his fingers over the trigger. The shot was fired and it hit Yogendra on the left side of his chest. The impact of the bullet knocked Yogendra out and the last sound seemed to be that of the barrel. Yogendra saw darkness fill the depth of his eyes. His ears did not pick up any more action. He did not know where he was or what had happened to him. All he knew was being ushered towards a deep sleep. This did not, however, scare him. Yogendra was ready to see the light ushering him to the world of the dead. He was disappointed in not being able to deliver the message regarding a serious attack which could save several lives. However, the light never came. Yogendra may have prepared himself for death but the universe was not ready. The soldier completed his task and went about his way. When the soldier was leaving, his foot hit Yogendra's leg. Yogendra's leg had been pierced by bullets and blood was still spilling out of the wound. Even a little amount of touch had a huge effect on Yogendra's body at that time. The excruciating pain traveling up Yogendra's leg jolted him back to reality. He was not dead after all. Yogendra's body was warm and his mind awakened. He could not believe the things that were happening. Yogendra was alive after being shot on his chest. Initially, nothing made sense to him as it all seemed like a miracle. It was indeed a miracle that had still kept him alive after several injuries while the others were dead.

As his vision and mind cleared, Yogendra jogged his mind trying to find the logic behind the occurrence. Suddenly, it struck him that his pocket contained the locket given by his wife. While he was in action, the locket had broken from the string. Yogendra had kept it in his pocket to keep it safe. What he could not fathom was the locket saving him. The bullet had hit the locket and reflected back. The locket was made of metal as his wife had informed. This made him remember his wife's final words to him, "Lord Hanuman is always going to be with you and provide you strength. Please keep this close to you. My prayers will protect you from all dangers through this." Yogendra was grateful to his wife for giving him the locket. His wife's love and care had saved him from getting killed. No matter how hard he tried to find the logical reason, it was his destiny that kept him alive. Although he had never been religious, Yogendra's belief in universal power became stronger. There had to be someone rooting for him to step back from death.

The pain of the impact on his chest was consistent but Yogendra's mind was conscious. Every little drop of fear and uncertainty washed away from his mind. Yogendra's heart told him that the reason he was alive was that he was meant to be. His destiny had a lot more in store for him and he could not escape before completing his task. Yogendra believed that now that he was alive after the fatal attack, he would not die at any cost. The faces of his companions gave him the motivation to move. Yogendra had to act now to take the revenge he had been waiting for. He watched the soldier walk away with his walk towards Yogendra. The other Pakistan soldiers were standing at a distance, scattered in different directions. The young soldiers walked to join the group. Yogendra looked into his pocket. There was a single hand grenade left with him. To be able to utilize the weapon, Yogendra had to be precise. He had only one opportunity to get this right.

Yogendra, without a second thought, took out the pin from the grenade and aimed to throw it at the Pakistan soldier. Yogendra only had four seconds before the grenade would burst. He quickly threw it at the soldier and it fell into the man's jacket hood. When the Pakistan soldier felt a sudden movement on his coat and a sound of an object, he turned to look behind him. To his surprise, there was no activity. There were two riffles on both his shoulders which restricted his movement when he tried to fish out the object. The soldier did not know what article had fallen into his hood but he could feel the weight. He moved his hand around the hood but could not reach inside to pry out the grenade. By that time, it was too late and the grenade exploded. Yogendra watched the back of the young soldier's head get divided into several small particles and the body fell near his foot. The body was disfigured and the clothes were torn. His face was completely smeared and spoiled and could not be recognized.

As soon as the rest of the Pakistan troop heard the explosion of the grenade, there arose a commotion within them. They had reignited doubts that someone, among the Indian soldiers, was alive. The Pakistan troop had already walked quite some distance down the slope and the vision of the landing was completely barred for them. They had already checked and shot the Indian soldiers twice. They could not have been alive but the grenade could not be overlooked. This created confusion in their minds. Yogendra knew this doubt would not be good for his safety. If the Pakistan soldiers returned to check, they will make sure every soul is dead. Then is when it struck him. He had to distract them and give them a different idea to chase. Yogendra noticed a rifle on the ground, well within his reach. He instinctively held out both his hands to pick it up. Within a moment his left hand did not move. Yogendra was shocked and persisted to move it and grab the gun on the ground. His trials failed as his hand was majorly injured. The bones of his left hand had been dislocated and broken and the nerves had been severed. Despite such grave injuries, Yogendra willed himself to pick up the weapon.

Yogendra decided he would do it with one hand if he had to. With all the strength in his body, Yogendra picked up the gun with his right hand and pulled the trigger. The shot was not directed at a target. It was a sweep around the area. He burst fired from one rock and then pushed his body to roll to the other side. Yogendra's broken and bruised body did not move easily. He let it fall to the ground and roll to the other rock. Yogendra lodged another round of burst fire from that side. He continued to change sides and fire into the air. This strategy worked as the bullets from different directions suggested to the enemy that there were many Indian soldiers attacking from different directions. The idea of reinforcement was worrisome for the Pakistan soldiers. They were not going to stay back and get killed by a larger Indian troop. The Pakistan soldiers decided to leave and return with some other plan and more reinforcement.

Yogendra could see the enemy retrieving from the location. He wanted to follow their step but his body did not support him to stand up and walk. Yogendra was still not going to give up. He held on to the rocks and pulled himself. He crawled towards the edge of the landing. Yogendra watched the Pakistan soldiers walk towards what looked like their camp. Pakistan soldiers were sitting around tents and food was being prepared. Without his knowledge, Yogendra had actually reached close to the Tiger Hill top. The top bunker was only a few feet away. Yogendra observed the location and the Pakistan soldiers. Yogendra was alone on the landing and this was the only peaceful time he had received in hours. He rested near the edge for a while, looking at the Pakistan soldiers doing different tasks. This was Yogendra's time to contemplate and re-energize himself to be able to escape and call for help.

XIII
Fortune's Child

1600 hours, 4th July 1999

Yogendra had only one mission in his mind and that was to inform his superiors about the impending attack being planned by the Pakistan army. He wanted to save his companions. Yogendra crawled back to the place where his fellow soldiers lay dead. It then occurred to him that some of the other soldiers may be awake, just as him. Yogendra already knew that Tarun and Anantram were dead. He went to the other soldiers around the bunker with the hope to find someone alive. His expectation was broken as he went closer to them. Yogendra could not stare at their bodies for long. Most of them were disfigured and scarred. Yogendra crawled near the bodies of the soldiers. Some men had only half of their faces existing while the other half disintegrated. The others had their lungs and kidneys out of their bodies after being shot several times. The sight of his dead companions finally hit Yogendra hard. He had been putting up a brave front for a long time but the tattered condition of his men broke Yogendra's resolve. Tears rolled down his eyes and did not for a long time. Yogendra cried his heart out. It felt as if a barrage had been broken as he had never experienced it before.

Yogendra crawled towards Singh's body, hoping for his friend to be alive. The last time Yogendra had seen Singh, he had lost some blood from a grenade injury but he was alive. Yogendra pushes himself towards his friend's body that now lay flat on the ground. Yogendra touched Singh's hand and it had turned extremely cold. There were several holes on Singh's chest and abdomen. Blood had seeped out and wet the shirt completely. Tears did not stop falling from Yogendra's eyes. He had lost two of his closest friends in the war and many more other companions. Yogendra could not swallow this information. The fatal injuries on Yogendra's body and the intense emotional release called in the fatigue. His body laid against the rocks while his eyes stared at a distance. Yogendra's body was catching up to the loss of blood. After crying for so long, Yogendra felt shivers run down his body. He began to feel extremely cold. Yogendra wondered if it was death, turning his body cold.

Yogendra sat near a rock and attempted to gather himself. He had to control his tears as his body shivered severely. The dislocated bones on Yogendra's left hand ended up clashing against each other with minor movements in his body. The clashing of the bones caused unbearable pain for Yogendra. He decided to tie his hand around his neck to restrict the movement. They did not have any medical equipment, so Yogendra tore his bandana with his right hand using a rock. He then brought his left hand close to his body and circled the cloth around. Yogendra was tolerating the pain to achieve a temporary solution to his problem. However, the shivers running down his body did not allow his hands to be steady. He could not tie the knot even after several trials. The left hand did not have any stability. It moved as many times as Yogendra tried to bring it close. To Yogendra it seemed to have been broken, so he decided to detach it from his body. This would give him free access and dissipate the pain that had become excruciating. Yogendra held on to his left lower arm and pulled it hard. Severe pain shot up his arm but Yogendra did not make any noise. He took several attempts to pull out his arm from his body. However, it did not work and the arm remained in place, causing more pain.

Yogendra found the ultimate solution in a while. His arm was dislodged from the sockets, so he threw it behind his back. The immobile hand was causing a lot less pain with this solution. Yogendra used his right hand to lock his fingers at the back of his belt. Yogendra began to think about his escape route. He wondered if a boy of nineteen with two years of service experience was supposed to have all the answers. Yogendra did not have experience on his side. The route that had taken was completely unknown. The senior officers had guided them to make the journey in the night. Therefore, Yogendra had no clue about the direction. It had started getting dark now, all Yogendra could see were the mountains surrounding him. It is to be believed that an honest heart has the power to build its own destiny. Yogendra sat near the rock and contemplated the outcome of the day. He wanted to save himself and the others but he did not know the way to return. However, he was not ready to give up and so was the universe. Right then Yogendra's eyes landed on a small channel(naala) on the mountain. He did not ponder much upon the consequences as he heard an eternal voice advising him to slide through the slope.

Yogendra felt that the channel was his only way of escape. He followed the divine calling and released him into the channel. Yogendra, initially, attempted to slide through the slope. Almost half way, his body caught up to the momentum. It started to roll down the slope. Yogendra was not in control of the descent anymore. He had left all his hope with the universe. Yogendra noticed a hole in front of him. Falling in the pit would end up breaking his other leg. Yogendra was short of a hand which made it even more difficult to stabilize his body. He could see the pit coming closer as his body kept on rolling over the slope. Yogendra groveled to hold on to something on the ground to stop the downward movement. When he had almost reached the edge of the slope, Yogendra's hands luckily got hold of a rock. He held on to the rock with his right hand. Having the entire body weight on one hand made it extremely painful. The injured leg was able to provide any support as it glided over the slippery slope. Yogendra's right hand was so pumped that it felt as if his tendons were slowly tearing away. His shoulder and leg had to bear the impact of the descent. The pressure on the injured areas led to more blood lose. Yogendra tolerated the pain still without any crying or screaming. He hoped for some help to appear for him. Until then, Yogendra closed his eyes and held on to the rock for dear life.

It had been a long slide for Yogendra. He had lost any idea about his location. For a moment, it occurred to him that he might have breached enemy territory. This would only result in being captured and killed. Yogendra had learnt about many soldiers who had been taken as captive by the enemy. They would torture the Indian soldiers to accumulate information and finally kill them whether or not the purpose was achieved. All this was circling in Yogendra's mind when he suddenly noticed Indian uniforms a few meters below. The men in his team who had not been able to climb the ridge and reach the landing were waiting for new orders. During the attack, the soldiers waiting below had also been hurt by the impact of the bombing. They could not climb onto the landing till the very end due to the continuous firing. The group had also logically assumed that none of the soldiers on the landing would be able to survive after the attack. After they noticed there were no changes in the situation, they had decided to walk back to the MMG post and summon reinforcement. At that moment, Yogendra felt that God himself was reaching out to him and offering his hand for help. It was no less than a miracle to see his team member near him at the same time that he got stuck at the edge of the slope. Timing was in Yogendra's favor throughout the mission.

Yogendra screamed to call out to his companions but no one responded. He went twice and thrice. Suddenly it occurred to him that his screams had very little sound. Yogendra had not spoken to anyone for hours. He had to pretend to be dead which meant complete silence. Yogendra had not even had any food or water since the last break on the morning of July,3rd before climbing up the ridge. His voice was hoarse and dry which demanded water. This led to very soft sounds escaping from his mouth. His body had become too weak to gather the energy to speak. As Yogendra watched his team moving further away, something clicked in him. He knew all the pain he had tolerated would be of no value if he failed to utilize this moment. Moreover, it was also the lives of his companions which had been lost that needed justice. Not only had the soldiers who were dead but also had the ones alive needed Yogendra to be alive so that he could deliver the crucial information to his seniors.

Yogendra mustered up all the strength in his body and gave out a loud hark. In the meantime, he also had to be careful enough to hold up his body on the slope without causing more damage. One of the members turned to trace the sound. He stopped the senior officer, "Sir, I hear a voice calling us out." Yogendra continued screaming to attract the attention of the soldiers. The others heard the sound in no time. When one of the soldiers saw movement on the slope and his eyes landed on Yogendra's form, he imagined he had seen a ghost. The figure seemed to be familiar but it was impossible for someone to be alive. The entire team had already analysed the situation and concluded that there could be no trace of life. After listening to the cry for help, one of the senior officers enquired, "Who is it?" Yogendra replied as loudly as possible, "Yogendra, Sir." The officer continued his questioning, "Which Yogendra?" Yogendra was instantly reminded of his friend Singh's demise. They were identified in the team for sharing their name. Yogendra informed, "The younger one, Sir BRAVO YADAV."

The officer ordered the soldier, Sunil, "Go ahead and check. We need to rescue him if our soldier is alive." The soldier climbed a few meters and noticed Yogendra hanging on the edge of a slope with the help of a rock. His clothes were completely tattered on all sides. Blood stains made the uniform darker. Even from far away Yogendra's injuries appeared grave. The soldier went ahead and offered his hand to Yogendra. However, Yogendra could not take the offer as his left hand was damaged and right hand was holding the rock. He shook his head, "My hand is broken and has no movement. You will have to pull me." Even though Yogendra's voice was feeble, there was clarity in his words which meant that he was conscious. The soldier nodded, "Don't worry let me get you out of here. It might hurt." The words appeared almost funny to Yogendra who had surpassed all physical pain in the last few hours. The pain that he was struggling with most was the mental one. The soldier held his right hand and supported his body to get off the edge. Then he picked Yogendra and brought him to the slope.

As Yogendra was brought to a plain area, he looked at the face in front of him. It was Sunil, another soldier from the grenadiers. It felt surreal to watch a face that looked back at him. Being stuck with the dead for hours had been menacing. Even in his nightmares, Yogendra had not imagined watching his own companions and friends lie dead for hours. Sunil's hands were not cold and his eyes had the life that Yogendra had almost lost. There was shock on both their faces. Yogendra watched as Sunil fumbled to fix his makeshift bandages. Sunil uttered, "I am not sure how to hold you. There seems to be injuries over all the parts." Yogendra did not know what to tell Sunil. He was in awe of hearing another voice that belonged to his home. Sunil understood Yogendra was still processing his surroundings and did not pry him with questions. He knew Yogendra would be bombarded with enough queries by the senior officials in no time. Although Yogendra was taking his time, he was nowhere disoriented. All Yogendra did was signal with his hands towards the downward slope where the team had halted after hearing Yogendra's voice.

Within seconds the restlessness in Yogendra's body increased as if he was in a hurry. Sunil called out to the other soldiers, "We have got one alive here. It is Yogendra Singh Yadav. He is badly hurt. I need help here." The other soldiers from the Ghatak Platoon, Delta Company and 18 Grenadiers came running a few meters upwards. They noticed Sunil sitting by Yogendra who was lying flat on the ground. The impact of the grenade had torn Yogendra's uniform. The scars in his body were clearly visible. Watching Yogendra living and breathing was surprising for all the soldiers. The attack was so massive that it had taken down all the Indian lives on the landing. Among all of them Yogendra had managed to escape and this looked like a true miracle. Yet there were doubts regarding his survival. Yogendra's severed condition did not indicate a positive outcome. The wounds on his body were deadly and the team did not think it was possible for anyone to recover from such fatal injuries.

JCO Sagar, a young officer, came forward and kneeled beside Yogendra. He consoled, "Don't worry! You will be just fine." Although the other soldiers did not have much optimism left after watching Yogendra's condition, the officer believed in his strength. Yogendra, however, did not care about any of it at the moment. He continued to utter the same sentence again and again as if it was a loop stuck in his mind. Yogendra pleaded, "I will be fine, Sir. All our soldiers are dead. Please save the post." Initially, his words did not make sense but as Yogendra kept repeating it, the words became clear. The soldiers understood that there was some danger looming upon the MMG post. However, the JCO did not pry Yogendra for more information. He understood that Yogendra needed immediate medical assistance which was more important. Witnessing Yogendra's condition highlighted the situation faced by the men on the landing. It pained him to think of the loss endured by the nation for losing the best of its men. In situations such as these, Sagar felt helpless in not being able to do anything to have saved the lives of the young men.

The other soldiers experienced similar emotions as they related to Yogendra's situation. It may very well have been any of them in his shoes or worse join the ones who were dead. The thought of so many men dead did not sit well with the soldiers. It immediately steered their minds towards their own deaths and the effect of the consequence on their families. It was strange to see Yogendra not being concerned about any of it. All he cared about at that moment was to save the post. Most men wondered if such a crisis transforms a person into being this fearless. As he had seen death so close, Yogendra was not stirred by the idea of it. It may have been his heart that gave him the strength to be so selfless. All his thoughts were directed towards the well-being of his nation. Yogendra was ready to sacrifice his life in a heartbeat to achieve the goal of saving the country. In that moment, Yogendra filled the other soldiers with pride and inspiration. Many of them may be dead but one of them was alive. It may have looked like a miracle but the soldiers were certain that it could not be possible without Yogendra's determination.

JCO, Sagar ordered, "Remove the remaining uniform on his body. We need to look at the injuries." One the soldiers began cutting the already torn shirt. It could not be removed from his body without cutting. The torn pieces of clothing stuck to Yogedra's skin from the mixture of blood and dust. Removing the pieces caused a stinging sensation for Yogendra. The soldier was cutting the coat pieces and throwing them away. Even in pain, Yogendra did not lose his humor, "Sir, please don't throw away the uniform pieces." Everyone was confused as to why Yogendra was concerned about the uniform at that moment. JCO, Sagar asked, "Is there something wrong?" Yogendra replied, "Sir, don't throw away the coat. I will have to bear the cost. My Quarter Master has strictly asked us to return the coat or we will have to pay the penalty. So, I have to return this anyway." Yogendra's statement suddenly elevated the tension. People shared a light laughter watching the young man's carefree nature. Sagar reasoned, "You are one strange man. You are on the brink of death and yet you are concerned about the coat. You do not need to worry about the uniform now. There are more important things on your priority such as your life."

Yongerdra's pants and shirt were removed next, leaving him in his undergarments and boots. The cold temperature was unbearable which made the wound shrink and cause more pain. There were many splinters inside his clothes which had not pierced the body. Yogendra was given a new coat to protect himself from the cold. After a few feet, Yogendra was made to sit by a rock with another soldier from his team. The other soldiers went about preparing to evacuate Yogendra to provide him medical assistance. Ram, sitting beside Yogendra, stared back at him and his injuries. Slowly tears began to fall from his eyes. Yogendra questioned, "Why are you crying?" Ram rubbed his face, "I am afraid you will not survive from the injuries. I feel terrible to see you in this situation. We have so many companions together. I do not want you to die." Yogendra pat Ram's shoulder, "I am not going to die. Don't worry, I am completely alright." Ram nodded, "Promise, you won't give up even if you see a bright light approaching you?" Ram's innocence had always impressed Yogendra. They had been through the entire journey together, since their training at the academy. It was heartbreaking for Ram to see Yogendra fighting death.

Ram's simple statements reminded Yogendra of Amarjeet. If his friend had been there, he would have cracked several jokes to distract Yogendra from his pain. Yogendra was facing mixed feelings. On one hand the memories from his training days provided him some respite and on the other hand the loss of his companions caused him pain. Memories often have this dual effect on people. Yogendra was dwelling on his memories, when Ram shook him, "Stay awake, brother." Yogendra realized that he was dozing off. He requested Ram, "I am fine. Can you please give me some water?" Ram shook his head, "I can't do that. I have been asked not to give you water and keep an eye on you. These are the orders of the JCO. We cannot risk the poison spreading in your body due to the water. I have to keep you awake. You need to keep patience." Ram could sense Yogendra's growing agitation as he could neither rest nor drink water. Yogendra had never felt so parched. The entire desert had landed on his mouth. To Yogendra it felt as if he could drink an entire ocean if he was given a chance. Yogendra, however, tried to control his thirst.

Yogendra was addicted to another habit of chewing tobacco. He knew this could temporarily distract him from his pain. Yogendra reached out to his sole companion, "Fine you don't want to give me water but do you have some tobacco?" Ram looked at Yogendra with disbelief, "You are dying here and you care about having tobacco at this hour." Yogendra laughed, "If I am dying, I would rather do so on my own terms. I know you must have some with you. Come on spill." Ram agreed to give some tobacco after hesitation. Yogendra's mouth was too dry to take in the tobacco. He picked up some ice from the ground and rubbed it against his lips. The droplets of water entering Yogendra's mouth tasted bitter which was a result of the dirt and blood all over his hands and face. Yogendra then accepted the tobacco from Ram, "Could you maybe prepare it for me?" Ram's stare was enough to tell him that the answer was a no and his companion did not appreciate his choice at the moment. Yogendra put the tobacco leaves over the coat that he was wearing. He then continued to grind it with his thumb until it turned into small particles. Once he placed the mixture into his mouth, Yogendra stated, "Now that would be a better death."

Yogendra's lighthearted candor surprised and impressed everyone. He kept his calm even in the worst situation. The other soldiers knew that he may not survive, considering his wounds yet Yogendra's will to live was so strong that it allowed everyone to remain positive. Yogendra's wounds were tended and temporary bandages were put around the gunshot wounds. Every time the white bandage was wrapped, it turned to red. The blood loss could not be stopped. They wiped the area clean and kept it under wraps. After a while, the soldiers came and informed them that it was time to take Yogendra to the base. Some of them picked up Yogendra and descended the slope. They had already informed the CO Kushal Thakur about Yogendra's condition. They did not have any equipment such as stretchers to take Yogendra back. The CO ordered back, "Bring back the young man as soon as possible. We cannot wait anymore. You should start the journey towards the camp. I am sending the reinforcement. They will meet you halfway and take over."

As promised, almost after reaching half the way, the team saw reinforcement along with stretchers and sleeping bags. Yogendra was put inside the sleeping bag and carried till the post. It took those two and half hours to reach the base. By that time, Yogendra was on the verge of losing consciousness and had completely lost his vision. He could not see or identify anything apart from sudden bursts of light. The temporary loss of sight was due to the heavy blood loss. Yogendra was directly placed on a bed and people began tending his wounds. Doctors were giving instructions to the assistants while they went about opening the bandages and accessing the wounds. Yogendra could only feel people walking around him and listen to them speaking in hush voices. Suddenly, there was complete silence in the room. Yogendra felt someone sitting on his bed. Then came a voice, "Can you recognize me, son?" The voice was calm and composed. Yogendra felt at peace with the person sitting next to him. He replied, "I am sorry, Sir. I am unable to see anything."

CO Kushal Thakur moved closer and pat Yogendra's hand, "I am your Commanding Officer, Lieutenant Kushal Thakur. Don't worry you are going to be fine." Yogendra nodded, "I am not worried about myself, Sir. You must save the post." CO Kushal Thakur wondered, "You are still worried about the post while you lay here fatally injured." Yogendra smiled, "I will be alright, Sir. Could you help me with something?" The CO eagerly asked, "Yes, son. Tell me what you need?" Yogendra managed with a hoarse voice, "I am feeling very cold, Sir." CO Kushal Thakur could see the goose bumps on Yogendra's hand and his body shivering rapidly. The commander immediately ordered the soldiers to light up a fire near Yogendra. This quickly warmed up the room. Yogendra started to feel the heat within five minutes. The warmth brought his mind back to his thirst. Yogendra felt thaf he would die without the water. It had been more than twenty four hours that he had any liquid to drink. It was time to ask for help and so Yogendra did. He called out to the CO, "Sir, I need one more help. Please give me some water." The CO shook his head, "I cannot give this to you soldier. You already know the protocol. We cannot risk the poison spreading in your body. We still need time on our hands to shift you to a bigger hospital."

The doctor heard the conversation from the other side of the room. He picked up a bottle of glucose and moved towards Yogendra. The doctor then opined, "There are no risks of the poison spreading now. You can drink some of the glucose." Yogendra was never so happy to hear something. The doctor handed over the bottle to Yogendra. The men watched as Yogendra chugged down the entire bottle in seconds. He felt a sudden surge of energy and that life had entered back into him. The one letter drink was absorbed by his parched body in no time. He remembered the last time he shared tea with his team. Singh had helped him prepare it. Yogendra had not known that it would be their last mail together. His eyes turned wet again as the thoughts circled in his mind. Yogendra had never shed tears in his life and now they were not ready to stop as if a barrage had been broken. The doctor moved ahead and cleaned Yogendra's broken arm. It was then put in a temporary splint. Yogendra patiently waited for the doctor's instructions to move in the direction they asked. Yogendra still could not see, therefore, sound was the only form of guidance.

After the doctor was done with the initial treatment, Yogendra was left with the commanding officer. CO Kushal Thakur enquired, "Would you like to tell me what happened up there?" Yogendra felt the tears brimming on his eyelids, "We have lost a lot, Sir. I saw my companions die in front of my eyes. In spite of the shortcomings, we gave a big fight. We defended ourselves for hours. Not all is lost. The next attack will be on the MMG post. You will have to protect it, Sir." The commanding officer did not take away his eyes from Yogendra's face. Yogendra narrated, "They had opened fired at us before all our soldiers could reach the landing. Seven of us kept on counter attacking the opponents. We managed to capture their bunker. The fight became difficult for us as our ammunition was limited. We managed to kill the Pakistan soldiers sent to survey the area and took over their weapons. However, things became tough when the Tiger Hill base camp launched an attack on us. All my companions perished one after another. I pretended to be dead to be able to survive. I heard the Pakistan officer talking about the next attack. They noticed our MMG post and wanted to eliminate any risk of future attack. I had only one goal, which was to come back and deliver this information."

Yogendra continued to provide every minor detail to the CO while he silently heard everything Yogendra needed to say. The company had lost seven men in that attack. CO Kaushal Thakur questioned, "Can you point out the exact location of their base?" Yogendra nodded, "Sir, their base is visible from our post. It is directly on top, adjacent to our post. Their MMG post is right beside their tents." Yogendra heard someone entering the tent. CO Kushal addressed the man, "He is still conscious but eye sight has not returned." The man spoke to Yogendra, "I am your Second in Command, D.B.S Pangal. Do you remember me?" Yogendra confirmed, "Yes, Sir. I do." Pangal went ahead and added, "We are trying our best to get you accurate medical treatment. You have to keep patience and hope." Yogendra knew hope is all that has kept him alive. CO Kushal equired, "Yogendra, could you tell me the requirement of the soldier on the field?" Yogendra replied, "We need ammunition and medical equipment like field stripes." The CO questioned, "How many weapons and medical stripes were you assigned?" Yogendra answered, "We had one personal weapon and one field stripe each. That became a problem when all the soldiers were hurt." 2IC Pangal asked, "Don't the soldiers need food and ration on the field." Yogendra smiled, "We do not feel hungry on the battlefield. It has been seventy two hours since we had eaten half a packet of biscuit and tea. Since then we did not feel any need for food. All we need are resources to protect ourselves."

After the conversation with the officers, one of the doctor's assistants came to give him proper clothes. By this time Yogendra's vision had recovered. Although it did not have perfect clarity, Yogendra could see his surroundings. He got adjusted to the objects and people in the room. Yogendra was most scared about losing his sight. Relief washed over him to be able to finally see things. The nursing assistant helped him wear the clothes. He then moved on to Yogendra's shoes. When the soldier attempted to pull Yogendra's shoes, it got stuck. Yogendra suggested, "I think there is something stuck on my shoes. Please check." The nursing assistant checked and pulled out a splinter from Yogendra's leg. His shoe was filled with blood which spilled from the shoes. The nursing assistant commented, "How have you been walking mate. This is a pool of blood. Hold on, let me patch it up." After the dressing, the doctor came into Yogendra's room along with another visitor. Yogendra recognized the man to be his first company commander, Major Rajiv Kumar. The man looked as polished as he did on the first day of Yogendra's service. Major Kumar enquired, "How are you feeling soldier?" Yogendra respectfully replied, "I am fine, Sir." Major Kumar was inquisitive about the young man in front of him, "When did you join service, boy?" Yogendra answered, "I started in January 1998 under your leadership in Kharu." Major Kumar was surprised, "So, you recognize me?" Yogendra nodded, "Yes, Sir. You were my company commander. We have had formal introductions." Major Kumar smiled, "I am sorry soldier. I do not remember you but you have done great work today. You will be absolutely fine."

Yogendra was happy to see a familiar face after a long period of uncertainty. After the Major left, the doctor gave Yogendra an injection which made him drowsy. He could not do much except see people carrying him out of the tent. All the people he knew came close to his stretcher saying things. Yogendra could not hear any of it. His mind was back in a trance. All he did was utter the same words in a loop, "All men are dead. Save the post." CO Kushal came close to him and touched his arm, saying things that did not register but his aura seemed to calm Yogendra. CO Kushal's reassurance and the effect of the medicines transported Yogendra into the land of tranquillity. War changes everyone yet it was surprising to see a nineteen year old boy turn into a man overnight. The young man had been changed for life by this incident. The maturity in his narration was evident to the commander. He had lost a lot on this journey which had strengthened his resolve. This had also broken his heart and given him a lesson in life. Yogendra showed not only strength but also wisdom. He tolerated pain and also strategized intelligently when it was needed. The information that Yogendra had carried was crucial to the battle. CO Kushal Thakur knew that the prior information regarding the attack provided the Indian army with a leverage against the Pakistan army.

XIV
Second Life

Yogendra's eyes opened to the fan on the ceiling. He attempted to get up from the bed as his eyes adjusted to the surroundings. However, his body did not support his endeavour. He settled back on the bed with the growing pain. The lower portion of his body was completely immobile and the upper portion did not make it any easier. Yogendra watched his body covered in several bandages and very little skin was visible. From the presence of patients around him, Yogendra knew that he was in a hospital but he did not have any idea about the location. The last thing Yogendra remembered was being escorted out of the tent on the post. CO Kushal Thakur was there to supervise the activity. Yogendra remembers being given an injection which made him drowsy. After this incident, he did not remember what had happened or how long it had been since he had been asleep. The bandages on his body told him there had been operations but try as he might, he could not remember anything.

When Yogendra saw the nurse, he excitedly attempted to sit up. He knew she could give him the answers to his questions. When the nurse noticed the agitated movement, she ran near Yogendra's bed, "What do you think you are doing, soldier?" Yogendra did not answer the question, "Where am I? How long have I been here?" The nurse put her hand on Yogendra's right shoulder, "First, you need to lie down peacefully. Then you can get your answers. You have given us enough trouble. Come on now, be good." The nurse had a motherly commanding tone and Yogendra immediately followed the instructions. He laid peacefully and repeated his questions, "Where is this hospital? How long have I been out? What about the war?" The nurse replied, "Hold your horses son. You are at the 92 base hospital in Srinagar. You have been unconscious for three days. There were several gunshot and splinter wounds over your body. The situation was very complicated in your case. The doctors had been working on multiple injuries. The result could have been a touch and go but the odds were in your favor. I will now have to go and inform the doctor that you are awake."

Yogendra stopped the nurse, "Wait a minute. What about my family?" The nurse assured, "You will be transferred to the Chandigarh base hospital. Then you can meet your family." Yogendra shook his head, "No, I cannot go to Chandigarh. My family will not be able to come down there." Then the nurse looked at Yogendra in confusion, "We are sending conscious people to other base hospitals. The casualties are transported on alternate days. They are sent to Udhampur on Tuesdays, Chandigarh on Thursdays and Delhi on Saturdays. What do you want us to do?" Yogendra replied, "Please send me to the nearest hospital in Delhi. My parents will be able to visit me there." The nurse nodded, "Alright, we will prepare for your transfer to the Delhi hospital on Saturday. Now I need to call the doctor and he will conduct the daily check-up. Do not even think about moving from that position on the bed if you do not wish to break your bones again." With that statement the nurse left the room. Yogendra remembered how painful it had been breaking his bones the first time. Although there was still pain all over his body but nothing in comparison to what he had experienced during the mission.

After the nurse had left, Yogendra lay in his bed recollecting the events of the past few days. His mind went back to the gunshots and bombings. The blood bath on the field and the faces of his dead companions jerked him. Every scar on his body reminded him of the incidents that occurred. Strangely he could recall every tiny detail of the mission. Like pictures, it appeared on his inward eye. He even managed to remember the faces of his enemies that killed each one of the Indian soldiers. The thought made his blood boil and the questions rattled his mind. He had no idea if the Indian army was able to stop the attack on MMG post. No one was there to answer his questions. What disturbed him even more was the fact that he could not hold on till the end to fight for his nation. Yogendra was not sure if he could have taken these thoughts out of his mind without being sedated by the injections. The feeling of losing his friends, the loss and the pain did not let his mind experience any peace. His heart was also longing for his family and worried about their condition.

Just as Yogendra was lost in his musings, he was interrupted by a man. The man walked towards Yogendra, "I am in charge of the communication. The soldiers who are conscious are being given the opportunity to send a message to their families. Would you like to send a signal?" Yogendra replied hesitantly, "There is no telephone at my home." The operator asked, "Is there someone else you would like to talk to?" Yogendra remembered, "My brother is in the army. If you could call his unit then probably I can send him a message." The operator nodded and took the required information from Yogendra. Meanwhile, his mind went back to the conversation with the commanding officer. Yogendra had asked his CO, "Sir, I request you to not send a signal to my home if I lose my life in the war." The CO had enquired, "But why? Every soldier would want their family to know." Yogendra bowed his head, "My mother will not be able to handle the news." This statement was enough for the commanding officer to understand Yogendra's emotions. There was an incident in their battalion which had alerted him. Grenadier Praveen Kumar of Yogendra's unit had lost his life during the Tololing mission. His mother was the only member of his family who received the information through signal. His mother went into shock and could not accept the death of his son. She died before she could see her son's body for the last time. The villagers had to fulfil the last rites for Praveen. Yogendra had the same concerns for his family. He was the closest to his mother and did not cause any events causing pain in her life. Yogendra was doing everything in his power to protect his family.

When the operator called Jitendra's unit, Yogendra learnt that his brother had been away from the base for leave. This idea did not work for him. The operator looked at Yogendra's morose face, "Now? Is there any other way to send information to your family?" It then suddenly struck Yogendra, "Yes. I recall, my in-laws have a telephone at their house. Their house is not far from ours. Once they get the information, they can transfer it to my family." The operator dialled the number as instructed by Yogendra. After several rings, a man picked up the call, Yogendra enquired, "Hello! Can I speak to Mr. Om Prakash?" The telephone belonged to a neighbor who went ahead and called Yogendra's father-in-law. He came and picked up the receiver, "Hello! Who is this?" Yogendra replied, "I am Yogendra." There was silence over the call and then the man spoke, "Who Yogendra?" It had been two months since his marriage. Yogendra's father-in-law had only met him twice, so he could not identify his voice. Yogendra found the situation quite funny as he went ahead and explained, "I am Yogendra from Aurangabad, Reena's husband." Finally the man recognized him, "Sorry, I did not remember your name. What happened?"

Yogendra narrated, "I have broken my hand. I had a nasty fall while climbing on a mountain. Now I am in a hospital in Srinagar. I will be sent to the Delhi military hospital on Saturday. Please inform my family about my whereabouts and ask them to come and meet me." Yogendra's father-in-law grew concerned, "Is that all? Are you alright, son?" Yogendra tried to convince him, "I am absolutely fine. I hope you and your family are doing well." Yogendra's father-in-law interrupted, "We are all fine. Don't worry about us. You tell me about your condition." Yogendra wanted to be done with the conversation. He did not want to give out too much in the call which would only make his family sad. Yogendra replied, "I am fine. Thank you for receiving the call. I will not be able to stretch the call. We have been allotted only a few minutes. I hope you understand." The call ended after a few seconds with more warm wishes and concerns. He was relieved to have been done with the call and also to be able have some form of contact with his family. Yogendra's father-in-law, however, was not convinced. He was doubtful about Yogendra's condition and made it clear in his visit to his home.

On the same day, Om Prakash reached Yogendra's home. People in the house were busy with their chores unaware of the situation. Yogendra's mother noticed Om Prakash on the door, "Please, come in. I will call Reena." Om Prakash commented, "You must call everyone. I have some news." The tone of Om Prakash's voice did not make Yogendra's mother feel at ease. She quickly called everyone on the lawn. After the rest of the family gathered, Jitendra asked, "What happened uncle? Is everything okay?" Om Prakash started, "I got a call this morning. It was from Yogendra. He informed me that his hand was broken by slipping from a mountain. He is being sent to the Delhi base hospital on Saturday and wants you all to go meet him." Yogendra's mother was immediately worried about her son's condition, "Oh God! How did this happen? Is he alright?" Jitendra noticed the stress on his mother's face, "It is just a broken bone, Maa. He will be just fine." Om Prakash interrupted, "I do not think it was Yogendra." People got confused by this statement. Jitendra asked, "What do you mean uncle?"

Om Prakash took his time as this could be bitter for the family, "I do not think it was Yogendra's voice. It must have been someone else. Moreover, I don't believe it is just a minor fracture injury." This was enough to cause chaos in the family. Yogendra's mother sat down on the chair with her head dropping into her hands. Yogendra's father dropped the newspaper that he had been reading. Reena keenly looked at her father's face expecting more information on the context. Jitendra was the only one who had to manage the situation, "How can I be so sure about this? People do fall on the field and get hurt." Om Prakash nodded, "I hope that is the case but my heart tells me otherwise. This is such a big war and Yogendra was sent to a hospital for a minor injury. My mind does not settle with that explanation. Something doesn't feel right in this situation." Yogendra's family members became worried as the same doubts got transferred into their minds. Yogendra's mother insisted, "I want to speak to Yogendra. Jitendra, do something. You have to find out what is happening with your brother." Jitendra pretended to be composed but even he was worried about Yogendra's safety, "Do not worry. I will go and find out from the radar. We should all remain calm. I am sure he is okay."

Jitendra could not convince himself let alone anyone else. He could not wait another moment to know about Yogendra's condition. Jitendra went to the radar in Sikandrabad and connected to the control room in Udhampur. He was able to reach the Brigade unit after a lot of patience. Jitendra spoke to an official, "I need information regarding my brother, Yogendra Singh Yadav. He was posted in the Kargil war under the 18 Grenadiers Regiment." The official easily recognized the name from his data, "Yes, we do have him at the Srinagar base hospital. He had been shot on the field but he has recovered and remains conscious. He will be transferred to the Delhi base hospital tomorrow." Jitendra was instantly shaken, "Shot? You are sure he is well?" The official assured, "Yes, his condition is stable now." Jitendra was relieved and worried at the same time. On one hand Yogendra was safe which made him happy. On the other hand he was fatally injured which caused distress in his mind. Until he could see Yogendra with his own eyes, he would not be at peace. Now the bigger challenge was to return home and lie to his family. Releasing this information would only cause more stress.

Jitendra returned home to the entire family gathered on the lawn. Jitendra's mother ran towards him, "Is Yogendra well?" Jitendra strengthened his resolve, "Yes, Maa. He is absolutely fine. I just called his unit. They informed me that we will be able to meet him tomorrow in the Delhi base hospital." People seemed to breathe out in relief which they might have been holding on to. Everyone went about their tasks, preparing to go to Delhi. Jitendra's wife's eyes were locked on him. He went into their room avoiding conversation. He convinced himself that he was not lying, rather only telling half the truth. Yogendra was healthy, so people did not need to spoil their own health in the process. Jitendra's wife came into the room, "I know you are hiding something." Jitendra was taken aback, "No, there is nothing. I am just tired from the journey. Can you get me some tea?" His wife demanded, "You are not getting anything until you tell me the truth." Jitendra knew there was no use arguing with his wife, "Yogendra is stable. He had been shot but he is fine now. We have to keep this to ourselves. We cannot have people going into full panic mode." Jitendra's wife nodded in agreement, still trying to process the information. She wanted to ask more questions but they were interrupted by the sound of a visitor at their door.

They heard the movement and the door and noticed Reena standing with a shocked expression. During their intense conversation, they had missed noticing Reena standing at the door. They noticed her eyes brimming with tears which told them that she had heard the conversation. Jitendra's wife called Reena inside the room, "Reena, there is no need to worry. You heard your brother-in-law right. Yogendra is completely fit. We need to remain composed. Any bad news right now will only agitate Maa and affect her health." Jitendra added, "We are going to Delhi tomorrow. We can all meet him then and be relieved." Reena did not express, being true to her calm nature. However, she grew severely worried as time passed. Her mind kept rotating around the information. It had only been two months of their marriage and Reena did not even get to spend time with Yogendra. Now the thought of the man she was starting to know may not return caused intense misery. Reena buried the thoughts within herself, waiting for the next day to arrive when they could finally go and meet Yogendra.

Yogendra was extremely excited to be shifted to Delhi. The night had to pass and he will be closer to home. After Yogendra had traveled back to consciousness, his mind wandered around the thoughts of his family. He watched families coming to meet their sons. Yogendra waited for his turn to see his family. The three days of waiting seemed to be too long for Yogendra. He spent his time talking to the other men in his ward. There were so many stories from the battlefield that Yogendra learned. He shared his own tales with others that helped clear the cobwebs in his head. Yogendra was reminded of his teammates by the stories that he heard from the other soldiers. Occasionally, his mind went back to Amarjeet. He made efforts to not think about his smeared face lying on the ground. Probably, it was Amarjeet's doing that Yogendra got reminded of the final moments they had spent together. Amarjeet sitting by the tent was preparing food while Yogendra went about completing other chores. A conversation had somehow begun on the subject of food.

Yogendra and Amarjeet could debate on any topic. The two friends who talk for hours, pulling each other's leg. People could not handle the duo when they decided to make someone else their target of the day. The discussion about food landed on an argument regarding the supremacy of butter chicken and 'kadai' chicken. Yogendra reasoned, "Kadai chicken takes a lot more effort. You are just a scaredy cat who cannot handle spices." Amarjeet argued, "Why would I look at anything else when I have butter?" Yogendra did not need to answer the question, "Butter is your first love." Amarjeet laughed, "Thankfully, not the last one." He took out the purse from his pocket and stared at his wife's photograph, "This time for the holidays, I am going to take Lata for a vacation." Yogendra questioned, "Where do you think you would go?" Amarjeet smiled, "I always write to her about the beauty of the mountains. She wishes to see them and I would also enjoy experiencing it with her. I recall being so mesmerized when I had first reported at the Srinagar base. Probably, I will take her to Srinagar and buy her beautiful tulips. She loves flowers."

There was a look of longing on Amarjeet's face which was very rare and unusual from his humorous attitude. He had been married longer than Yogendra and had been away from home for a long time. Yogendra smiled at his friend's musing, "You do that and I will make sure you keep up on that thought." Amarjeet laughed, "Yes. Or else I give you the authorization to kick me. Come on now let's eat. You have been going about that work for a long time." Yogendra replied, "Coming in a few minutes. Let me keep the containers in place. Don't start without me." Amarjeet promised, "Never." Yogendra jolted back to reality every time he went through this memory loop. The days were gone but the memories were fresh in his mind. Yogendra still imagined Amarjeet waiting for him to start a meal. He strongly believed his friend was keeping his promise. It was his prayers and presence, along with his family and friends that saved Yogendra from the claws of death. Yogendra was certain that he may never find such a bond again in his life but the memories would be cherished forever.

Tiger Hill had been captured on 8th July, 1999 and the war was coming to an end. As promised, on Saturday Yogendra was being sent to the Delhi base hospital by flight. The bodies of the dead soldiers had been rescued and were being sent home by the same flight. Yogendra had no information regarding any of it. He was only excited to be able to meet his family after so long. The other Yogendra's body was also transported to Delhi by the same flight. Things went downhill when Yogendra reached the Delhi hospital. After settling into his ward, Yogendra got hold of a newspaper. There were several news articles on Kargil which was the main topic of discussion in the country. While skimming through the paper, Yogendra's eyes landed on an article in the corner of the first page. Yogendra's mind went blank as he read the news, "Martyr Yogendra Singh Yadav, 18 Grenadiers." This was the section which included the names of the soldiers who had lost their life in the war. Yogendra knew the letter was mentioning the death of his companion Singh but his family did not. Yogendra's mind instantly chalked the situation, considering his family either reads the paper or gets informed by some neighbor. Stress and worry filled his mind but there was nothing he could do anymore.

Yogendra's distress was not unjustified as the news did reach his home causing havoc in the household. The entire village went into mourning as the news spread that Yogendra had expired. People, however, missed the crucial detail regarding the martyred soldiers' city and district which could help differentiate the two Yogendra's. There was hardly any place for logic in that emotional storm. The villagers and relatives had gathered around the Yadav household. Yogendra's cousin came in with the news, "There is an article in the newspaper." The expression on his face and the vibration of his voice immediately made Jitendra think the worse. He already had information about Yogendra's injuries which may have aggravated. Jitendra enquired, hoping to hear something positive, "What is it?" The cousin could only muster one word, "Yogendra..." This was enough to shake the family. Jitendra pulled the newspaper out of his hands and frantically looked through it. As his eyes locked on the news, the paper slipped out of his hands.

Yogendra's mother could not hold her patience anymore. She went ahead and clutched Jitendra's hands, "Please tell me what is happening? Do not lie to me." There was no use lying anymore. Jitendra wanted to remain positive but he also had to be realistic. The entire village would know the news and it would travel to his mother. It was better for him to deliver the news to her and console her in the right manner. Jitendra stated, "Maa, Yogendra is no more." He did not know if there was a better way of saying this but his mother did not ask any question. Her body dropped to the ground. Jitendra sat down beside her, holding her. Within a second loud howling could be heard around the house. There was no stopping Yogendra's mother. No amount of consolation calmed her in the moment. His father, who was sitting on the chair in the corner, had several questions but at that moment could only manage his tears. Reena ran into her room, locking the door behind her. Jitendra's wife ran behind her, concerned about her safety.

The other relatives and villagers started coming to their house with questions of their own, "How did this happen?" Jitendra did not have any answer to this question, "We do not have enough details right now." The uncles and aunts sat beside his parents, consoling them, "Your boy was a hero, a true martyr." Jitendra was not ready for the word 'was' being used for his little brother. His resolve broke as tears rolled down his eyes. After a few minutes, Reena came out with Jitendra's wife. Her eyes were bloodshot red and her hair dishevelled for the bawling. She did not talk to anyone and her silence was not the usual one. There was misery written all over the peaceful young face. On the other hand, Jitendra's mother did not stop saying Yogendra's name. She kept speaking about her in between wailing. Jitendra had never seen such a bleak atmosphere at his house. He had to struggle a lot in his childhood but he had never felt so miserable. His heart dropped to his stomach. Jitendra's wife stood by him consoling him throughout the process.

The family received the information from the newspaper that the bodies were being sent to Delhi. The villagers enquired, "When are you going to bring the body?" Jitendra did not know how to react to that statement. His heart was not ready to accept that his younger brother was no more. The entire village was mourning the loss of the young boy they had all seen growing up among them. The villagers had left all their chores and waited for positive news. Most houses had not lit their stove and remained hungry the entire time. Jitendra's mother cried out, "I want to see my son. Bring him home to me, my sweet boy. He was in distress before he left. Yogendra had nightmares about the war. I shouldn't have let him leave. He could have been alive." Yogendra's father opined, "He is a soldier's son. No one could have stopped him. He was..." He stopped to recollect his thoughts and compose himself. He was not a man of many words nor expressions. When Jitendra looked lost, his father stated, "Prepare to go to Delhi and bring Yogendra home." His father's words brought Jitendra out of the trance. He had responsibilities to fulfil and manage everything at home. Jitendra, immediately, left for Delhi with his elder cousin. Both of them went to the RR hospital looking for Yogendra's information.

Jitendra and his cousin ran from desk to desk and ward to ward frantically. Even after hours, they could not find any leads on Yogendra. God may have been looking upon them when a familiar voice called out, "Jitendra? Is that you?" This was Jitendra's childhood friend Shankar who worked as a nursing assistant in the hospital. Jitendra was relieved, "I am here looking for Yogendra. We read in the news about his death." Shankar assured, "Don't worry. Let me look into the records." He went inside the administrative office and came back after a few minutes. Shankar informed, "Yogendra is not here. We must call the base hospital. They might have some news on him." They quickly connected to the base, and an operator picked the call. Shankar enquired, "I want information about a casualty named Yogendra Singh Yadav. His body may have been sent to the Delhi base hospital." The operator took his time, probably looking at documents, "Yes. We have one Yogendra Singh Yadav. He is majorly injured but conscious." Shankar was surprised, "Did you say he is conscious? He is not dead?" The operator replied irritated, "Yes. He is very much alive. You can come and see it for yourself." The phone got instantly disconnected.

Jitendra had heard Shankar's side of the conversation, "Yogendra is alive?" He was surprised by this news. Shankar nodded, "That is what the operator said. You must leave for the base hospital now." Jitendra's heart was right. Yogendra could not leave them so early. After all, he had always been so stubborn. Jitendra's cousin stated, "Let us just go and see. We will take it as it is." He did not want his young brother to be disappointed after raising his hopes. They reached the hospital in no time. Jitendra did not want to wait another second in meeting Yogendra. It was around five in the evening when they reached the destination. He rushed to the reception and was directed towards a huge ward. The large dorm had multiple beds with several patients. Jitendra's eyes could not trace the end of the large room from the doorway. They entered the room and started looking at every bed. There were soldiers covered in bandages wrapped all around their body. Their faces were mostly guarded by tapes which made it harder to identify. They had to look minutely as Yogendra might be asleep, not expecting them to be here.

Yogendra noticed his brothers before they could identify him. He called out to them from across the room. Jitendra recognized the voice but could not spot Yogendra. Then he noticed a frail man waving his hand at them. As Jitendra moved closer, he was surprised to see Yogendra. He had a long beard over his face and big hair on his head. His frame had become lean and his entire body was covered in bandages and plasters. Yogendra's face had several tapes covering the cuts. It was impossible to recognize him without his voice. It pained Jitendra to see his younger brother in this condition. As brothers they had never been expressive in showing their love. However, today Jitendra wanted to hug his brother. He was ecstatic to see his brother safe and alive. Yogendra had a big smile on his face, "How are you both?" Jitendra laughed, "We should be asking that to you, considering you are the one in the hospital bed." Yogendra replied, "I am fine. How is Maa?" Jitendra huffed, "She will be okay once we give her the news about you being alive. The article in the news had an ill effect on her. It got us all scared to our bones."

Yogendra nodded, "The article mentioned the name of my teammate. We shared the same name. He died on the battlefield. Is everyone else alright at home?" Jitendra sat on the corner of the bed, "Maa and Reena had the hardest time dealing with the news. It is never easy for anyone. You got us bad this time." Yogendra looked at his hand, "I can't imagine you being too scared." Jitendra laughed, "You could only know if you were the elder brother." Yogendra's cousin was observing the interaction, "What have you done with your face? You look like a hermit. You should get that beard cut or else no one will recognize you." The brother shared some more laughter and conversation. Yogendra asked his brother, "Are you going to stay the night in Delhi?" Jitendra replied, "People in the village have not eaten. They are all in mourning. Everyone has gathered in our house. We must return and give them the news. All those people need some relief." Yogendra felt sad to have caused such distress to his family. Jitendra added, "None of this is your fault. There was a miscommunication. You have fought like a brave shoulder and we are all proud of you. Everyone would like to meet you so we will be back soon."

Jitendra returned home in the evening with a lighter heart. Neighbours and relatives were still at his home waiting for his return. Jitendra shared the news with everyone, "Yogendra is absolutely alright and he is going to have a complete recovery." Jitendra's mother moved towards him, "You are telling the truth, right? My son is alive." Jitendra smiled at his mother, "Yes, mother. He is going to be just fine. Still being his humorous stubborn self." The news changed his mother's expression. The happy tears rolling down her eyes slowly dried up. Yogendra's father also looked relieved and had a huge smile which was only seen on rare occasions. The color had also returned to Reena's face. The bleak atmosphere of the house slowly dissipated. Jitendra promised to take everyone to see Yogendra on the next day. People went back to their homes with renewed hope. Now the Yadav family was waiting to meet their son as soon as possible.

XV

Survival

Jitendra had delivered the truth to all his neighbors and relatives yet they were not convinced. They wanted to see it for themselves to believe that Yogendra was alive. Several people of the village, along with Yogendra's parents, travelled to the Delhi base hospital in a pick-up truck. About twenty-five to thirty people gathered inside the hospital premises. Everyone looked at the large group of visitors in awe and wondered if someone popular had been admitted as a patient in the hospital. The nurses and guards blocked their entrance. Only two people were permitted to enter at the same time for a visit. Jitendra suggested, "Maa and Papa, you should go first. I will wait here with the rest of the people." Everyone agreed with the suggestion. One of the nurses guided Yogendra's parents, "Come with me. I will show you the dorm. Rest of the people, please maintain decorum inside the premises."

Yogendra's parents entered the dorm as pointed out by the nurse. Their eyes searched around the room, trying to spot Yogendra on one of the beds. Yogendra's bed was adjacent to the door which was out of their line of sight. Yogendra noticed some movement at the door beside his bed. He looked up and noticed his mother, "Maa?" Yogendra's voice could not be missed by his mother. Even with a long beard and wrapped in bandages, Yogendra's mother instantly recognized her son. As soon as she saw her son, tears rolled down uncontrollably from Yogendra's mother's eyes. Yogendra was sitting on the bed with his legs stretched. His mother rushed and sat beside him, wrapping her hands around her son. Despite the wounds,

Yogendra felt a sense of tranquillity which he had been missing. Only a mother's arms could provide such warmth that heals the wounds of the heart. She surveyed the wounds on Yogendra's body and continued to cry. Yogendra looked up at his father standing by the bed who also had his eyes wet.

Yogendra consoled, "Why are you crying, Maa? Look, I am fit." His mother wiped her tears, "You have been so hurt. You will understand a mother's pain." Yogendra felt terrible watching his mother in this condition, "I am going to be out of the hospital in a few days. Your crying is not going to help me recover. If there is some science to it, then I would also give it a try and start crying with you." Yogendra's mother touched his hand, "You are cracking jokes even now! You have no idea how difficult it has been for us. When we received the news that you were... I did not think I could survive this misery." Yogendra held his mother's hand, "I know, Maa but I am going nowhere. I will come home soon." Yogendra's mother shook her head, "There is no need to hurry. You are always very impulsive. I don't want you harming yourself during the recovery process. The doctor has said it is going to take time and you are going to listen to all his instructions without fuss." Yogendra's father agreed, "Listen to your mother. She wants the best for you. You need proper recovery. Any kind of hurry can delay the process. You need to rest well." Yogendra listened to his parents quietly, letting them speak their mind, considering how worried and scared they had been for the past few hours.

Yogendra asked his mother, "Where is Reena?" His mother stated, "She will be coming tomorrow with your sister. The house would be empty, so she stayed back. You have got her so worried. The new bride has only had bad experiences after her marriage. Such a sweet child had to endure so much. You have to now give her time and make her happy." Yogendra could not deny his mother's opinion. He, too, believed that Reena has had tough experiences since their marriage. Yogendra's duty towards his nation required him to move right after their marriage. They had only just begun to know each other. Yogendra knew he had similar responsibility towards his wife. It was important to give her the care she deserves as his wife. Yogendra's parents left the room with the promise of returning soon. After that people kept coming into his room. They had several questions and were all looking at him in surprise as if not believing if he was an apparition. Yogendra was the first soldier from the village to have actively fought such an important war and survived. People were simply happy to witness his recovery.

Yogendra waited the entire night to meet Reena the next day. There was not much activity the entire, other than sleeping on his bed. Therefore, meeting people appealed to him. Moreover, it was his newly wedded wife whom he had not seen for two months. In times of distress, thoughts of Reena also provided Yogendra with strength and motivation. He wanted to return home alive and fulfil his duty as a husband. Sharp at the visiting hour, Reena came in with Yogendra,'s younger sister. Yogendra's sister did not wait for pleasantries, "Have you got any idea how worried we were?" Yogendra had no idea what his fault was in the situation but arguing with an angry sister did not seem like the right choice. Yogendra's sister went on with her rant for about fifteen minutes. He knew it was out of concern and love for him, so he remained quiet. Yogendra's eyes drifted towards who stood silently by the bed. When Yogendra's sister noticed that the couple had not spoken a word to each other, "I will go get some tea. Reena, you stay and give him company."

After his sister left the room, Yogendra asked Reena, "You can sit on the bed. It won't break." Reena sat at the edge and inspected Yogendra's scars. Her eyes were puffy and red which meant she had been shedding tears for a long time. He noticed and stated, "It will heal. How have you been?" Reena did not answer the question as tears had already started flowing from her eyes. Yogendra often did not know how to handle such situations, "Please don't cry. Do I look so terrible?" Reena shook her head, seriously answering his question, "I was afraid that you will not return." Yogendra smiled at her innocence, "And I did return, didn't I?" Tears appeared more rapidly from Reena's eyes. Yogendra had only watched Reena cry at the 'vidaai' where her relatives were there to console her. He had never consoled a woman except her mother and the only way he knew how to tackle the situation was through humor.

Yogendra seriously added, "I think I can guess why you are sad." Reena was confused as to what Yogendra was trying to say. Reena only looked at him, waiting for him to continue. Yogendra stated, "I think you are sad because you will not get twenty-five lakhs." Reena was still unable to comprehend Yogendra's statement. He explained, "The government has announced an award of twenty-five lakhs for the families of the martyr. So, as I am not dead, you sadly will not get the amount. This must make you sad, right?" Reena finally understood Yogendra was joking, "How can you joke in such a serious situation and say such things?" Yogendra laughed, "Laughter keeps people healthy. So, you get me instead of the reward. I am not leaving so soon, so, I am sorry you are not getting the money." Reena looked flustered, "Stop it. Enough of your humor." He asked have you learnt to make Matar paneer from Maa, Reena smiled and said yes when you come home I will make for you. A laughter in between all three .They talked some more about home until it was time to leave.

People continued to come to meet Yogendra for the next few days. The Kargil war had ended on 26th July, 1999. Yogendra kept himself updated about the situation through the news on the television. He could not still leave his bed, so this was his only form of entertainment apart from chatting with people. On 29th July, 1999 Yogendra found a new visitor standing in front of his bed. The tall, lanky man looked at Yogendra curiously, "Are you Yogendra Singh Yadav?" Yogendra managed a nod. The man continued, "Commanding Officer, Kushal Thakur has sent a letter for you." He took out the letter from the pocket of his trousers and handed it over to Yogendra. The letter was kept inside a small envelope which contained Yogendra's name and address. Yogendra was surprised, "Letter for me? Did something happen?" The unknown visitor replied, "I have been asked to deliver this. The CO has asked everyone to meet the injured soldier on their way home who ever travels through Delhi. He said that you might get a lot of visitors from media houses and newspapers publishing establishments. You are instructed to learn the things written in the letter and narrate it when journalists come to meet you."

Yogendra read the letter after the man left. Although he did not agree with some of the descriptions, he read the letter multiple times for a few days. There were no more updates, so Yogendra forgot about the letter. Meanwhile, it had been a month that Yogendra had spent in the hospital. Yogendra's wife moved to a relative's house in Delhi to be able to meet him. His sister often traveled from Faridabad. Yogendra's initial humor had started to become dull. He was losing his patience and interest inside the hospital environment. Watching patients and medical staff had become monotonous for him. He was still unable to walk which trapped him to the bed. One day when the doctor came, Yogendra requested, "Doctor, it has been a month that I am stuck in this bed. Please tell the nurses to get me a wheelchair and roll me to the garden. I will be a good patient." Yogendra had become friendly with all the doctors and nurses. Everyone knew him for being stubborn but also funny and cordial. The doctor ordered the nurse, "You can take him to the garden in the evening but only if he takes all the medicines and follows his routine." The doctor turned towards him, "Your physical therapy is starting in two days, Yogendra, so be prepared."

Yogendra reminded the nurse as soon as the clock struck five, "Sister, please take me outside for a spin." The nurse could not deny Yogendra's cheeky smile. Two male nurses came in to help Yogendra into a wheelchair. Yogendra's wife, who had some for a visit, also joined them in the garden. Yogendra was finally out of the room. He was taking in the surroundings. It had been so long that he had smelled a fresh breath of air. Yogendra looked at all the beauties of nature around him. He opens his slippers and touches the grass with his feet. Yogendra felt much lighter and wanted to walk around the garden. He put his hands on the arm rest and pushed himself. The portion below his waste did not support him. His arms pumped up and Yogendra landed back in the chair. He hit the arm rest numerous times with his palm. The frustration was evident on his face. Yogendra had made several attempts over the month, trying to swing his legs down the bed. His injuries on the leg were so grave that there was very little strength left in them.

Reena was watching Yogendra's attempts from a distance. Lately, he had been quiet and disturbed. The feeling of incapability depressed Yogendra. Reena consoled, "Don't worry, it will get better in a few days." Yogendra sneered, "You have been saying the same thing for several days now." Reena had noticed this irritation in Yogendra from the past few weeks. He wanted to walk and get on with his life but his body was not ready to get back in shape. Yogendra had to take assistance to get his work done, whichever required movement. Being confined to the bed, also took his mind to the bad thoughts which pulled him even more towards misery. Reena often felt hurt by Yogendra's bitterness which only increased with time. More than anything, she was sad about his condition. Reena herself had requested the doctor to put Yogendra into physical therapy. The treatment was going to take time and recovery was slow. This was out of Yogendra's pattern as he never had the patience.

As physical therapy started, Yogendra started acting out. He was not the amicable guy for long. Reena was often scared to say the wrong thing in front of him. In the first session, Yogendra was completely uncooperative. He did think this was going to help him work. After multiple requests from Reena, he agreed, "I am only agreeing to this as you will stop pushing me once I agree." The doctor smiled and began performing different exercises on his leg. Yogendra was impatient about the process. When the doctor moved away, he attempted to stand again but like every instant he dropped down in the chair. The pain shooting up his legs was unbearable. His legs could not hold up the weight of his body. Yogendra screamed in agitation, "Why aren't you making me walk?" The doctor smiled, "That is a long way from hope, Yogendra. One step at a time. We need to get your muscles adjusted to activity first." The doctor's words made sense but Yogendra was not in the right frame of mind to understand, "How long do you think you are going to take to do the job?" The therapist confidently replied, "If you do as I say, you will be walking within three weeks."

Yogendra would often lose his calm during the therapy sessions as he was unable to perform the activities on his own. He would have to take the support of the medical staff. Reena watched as Yogendra attempted to stand on his feet. Even a single step felt like a marathon. Yogendra felt needles piercing into his leg as he tried to stand. People holding him like a child made him feel extremely under confident about himself. Strength was one of his positive abilities. Now that he became dependent on people, he felt like a weak man. No amount of consolation was working with Yogendra. So, his therapist tried different techniques. He challenged and mocked him and this energized Yogendra. He was unable to see the progress he had made in two weeks. The man who was unable to stand was now taking steps with the help of a walker or an assistant. He was too miserable to see the positive sides of the situation. Yogendra challenged the doctor, "You had told me that I am going to walk in two weeks. It has already been two weeks, I don't see any signs of it happening." The senior doctor laughed, "We still have another week. Moreover, you refuse to look at the progress you have made. You are on your feet." Yogendra shook his head, "Yes, with someone's help. I want more progress than this. Depending on someone else is not a great feeling." The doctor assured, "Patience is the game changer."

Despite his hesitations, Yogendra continued his therapy. The process did calm him internally. The bitterness gradually dissolved. He felt like he was getting back to himself. Although there was still the frustration of not being able to walk on his own, the bleak clouds were clearing out. There was steady progress in his steps. One day Yogendra attempted to take a step by himself. Before he could do it, Reena was standing by his side forcing him back on the bed, "You are not trying this again. Follow the doctor's advice. Erratic movements can break the bone again. Take help from the nurses." Yogendra did not argue with his wife as it would not work. Reena had become comfortable around him, expressing his views more often around him. Reena was trying to protect and he understood her. However, Yogendra knew he had to push himself to achieve the ultimate goal. Therapy was definitely helping him but it was his spirit that could make him walk alone again.

Yogendra found his inspiration and the match to light the fire in his dorm. A soldier had been recently admitted after him who had lost both his hands. Initially, he struggled to survive but with time he managed to adjust with his situation. Yogendra had observed his journey. The soldier had not just managed but created an example. He was not dependent on anyone for his daily activities. He completed all the necessary chores by himself. Yogendra noticed the staff bringing food to the soldier. They did not feed him, rather he asked them to place a spoon on a strap that was tied on his arm. He got acquainted with the skill of eating food without his hands, along with many other activities. He did not want people to feel sorry for him. Yogendra thought to himself if a man in such a worse condition could remain positive and strive to be independent, then he definitely did have a better claim. Yogendra knew that the parts of his body were intact and that made it a lot easier for him, therefore, his complaints began to sound menial.

After Reena had left for home, Yogendra planned to try taking a step alone. The example of a child's first step circulated in his mind. A child learns to walk only by falling several times. Yogendra was not afraid to fall. He knew he had to take the risk to challenge himself. Yogendra motivated himself as he was the only player in his team. He swung his legs and touched his foot to the floor. The sensation of the cold floor felt comfortable on Yogendra's foot. He pushed himself with both his hands on the bed, supporting both sides of his body. Yogendra's destination was the bathroom. He had just taken a step towards the direction of the end point when he suddenly fell down. Yogendra's head became dizzy as he made contact with the floor. Yogendra's legs were shaking as he got up off the floor. The impact of the fall stretched the muscles on his leg and resulted in bleeding. His calves and arms pained yet Yogendra did not stop. During his trip to the washroom, Yogendra fell more than ten times but he did not give up. He reached the washroom, used it and came back to his bed. Yogendra had made it.

Yogendra did this activity every day when his wife or the medical staff was not in the dorm. As days passed, Yogendra's fall counts decreased. Yogendra learned to walk again like a kid. Yogendra successfully achieved his target with his determination. Both his wife and his wife were impressed by his fast recovery and progress. Reena commented, "Wow! You are doing so well. Have you been practicing?" Yogendra laughed, "A lot and alone. When we know there is no safety net, we give it our all to complete a task safely. Therefore, it was important for me to walk alone." Reena was concerned, "Still you should have had someone to keep an eye. Another fall could have broken a bone. It would have been terrible." Yogendra assured, "But nothing has happened. If we don't get up and try then how would we know if a task is possible?" Just as in the war, Yogendra's indomitable spirit helped him stand back up on his feet and walk again.

XVI
Honour

Yogendra had started walking by himself again. This gave him the opportunity to go around the hospital. Despite the nurse's disapproval, Yogendra went around different wards talking to people and learning new things. He did not have to wait for the medical staff to take him to the garden. He went outside whenever he wished. Although there were several restrictions, Yogendra did not pay any attention to them. His favorite activity was walking barefoot on the grass. Even if the nurses asked him to not go to the garden without the staff's assistance, he did not listen to any of them. The patients reminded him of the dead while nature reminded him of life. The sensation of the soft grass and sweet wind distracted him from the bleak thoughts and filled his mind with positivity. Apart from this, Yogendra enjoyed meeting new people and talking to them. Initial days had been lonely when he was in strict recovery. Yogendra slowly understood that through his interaction with people he would be able to engage his mind in the hospital. This would also help others to not lose calm due to idleness and share things with each other.

Yogendra had not been approached by any media house until the first two weeks of August, 1999. The journalist would often come to the hospital, trying to talk to the soldiers but Yogendra had never had any conversation with them. He usually avoided meeting with them like many other soldiers. In fact, when the journalist approached them, they were directed towards the Pahalwan who had a silver-tongue. He was very articulate and animated which helped in the engagement of people. The Pahalwan came up with loud, grand descriptions about the battlefield which the journalists appreciated. He loved talking to them and telling them his story with a lot more grandeur than warranted. The journalists gave him the attention he craved. It was a mutual understanding between both the parties. Yogendra, on the other hand, was never much of a conversationalist let alone a public speaker. Only recently, he had started talking more with people. However, speaking to the journalists gave him the jitters.

On 14th August, 1999 things began to change rapidly in Yogendra's life. He had just completed dinner and was sitting in the canteen. People had decided to watch the news. Yogendra was in conversation with one of the soldiers, "Today there were only two journalists, right?" Their conversation was regarding the journalists coming to the hospital. They had very less to talk about usually, considering very little was happening in their lives inside the four walls. Whenever new people came, they found topics to discuss. The soldier replied, "Yes but tomorrow there will be a lot more. I heard the nurses discussing that the national channel will be here, including us in a live coverage on the occasion of Independence Day." Yogendra laughed, "Certainly there is more love on this day." Suddenly, Yogendra was pulled towards the sound of the television. The news being narrated attracted his attention. The anchor repeated the announcement, "Four soldiers are being awarded with the prestigious Param Vir Chakra for their brave service in the Kargil war. The list includes three expired and one living soldier. Three posthumous awardees are Captain Vikram Batra of J&K Rifles, Lieutenant Manoj Kumar Pandey of Gorkha Rifles, Yogendra Singh Yadav of 18 Grenadiers, and Rifleman Sanjay Kumar of J&K Rifles, who survived the war."

Yogendra was ecstatic to hear that his friend and team member Singh had won such an honor. He represents the entire 18 Grenadiers and their core team which is a subject of immense pride. Yogendra looked at the soldier beside him and pointed towards the television screen, "Yogendra Singh Yadav was my friend. We fought together and he saved my life." Yogendra's heart filled with warmth with the memory of his friend. He would forever be in debt to Singh for helping him and guiding him throughout the journey. Most importantly, Yogendra knew he would not have been alive without Singh's intervention. The award that had only been part of stories that Yogendra had read was now being delivered to one of his own. Yogendra went about sharing the news with everyone in the hospital. He was ecstatic after a long time. Yogendra could not imagine how Singh would have felt if he had been alive to see this. Yogendra smiled to himself when it occurred to him that Singh, probably would have spent the day like any other, considering his simple and grounded nature. Rather they would have probably ended up cracking jokes and making fun of each other.

Yogendra remembered a conversation with Singh that he had on the last day of their fight after Singh had been shot. Yogendra was tending to Singh's wound risking his own life being in the line of fire. However, Yogendra did not worry as he had to save his friend at any cost. Between the loud panting, the men continued to speak to keep each other alert. Suddenly, Singh blurted, "The act that you are pulling off now, you think this is going to get you a Param Vir Chakra?" Being elder to Yogendra, Singh always scolded him whenever he acted impulsive. Yogendra jokes, "I am not the one with a bullet in my body." Singh laughed, "You might get one soon if you don't move fast enough." Yogendra nodded, "Almost done. Hold on there. It is no use if you get one and can't be there to see it." Singh smirked, "Death is the only inevitable end to the chakra of life." The recollection brought goose bumps on Yogendra's skin. Soldiers from all around the hospital came and congratulated Yogendra for his team's victory, "You must be so proud. One of you team members won the Param Vir Chakra for his regiment." Yogendra was indeed very proud and missed his companion more than ever.

Yogendra and the other patients had called off the night by eleven after an entertaining movie experience. At around two in the night, Yogendra felt someone tapping his arm. His natural instinct was to wrap his hands around the intruder and pin them down. As soldiers, they had been trained to always be vigilant. He was on the verge of attacking the person when he opened his eyes and noticed a nurse standing a few feet away. She had shifted her position noticing Yogendra's posture changing into one of attack. The nurse cautiously asked, "Are you Yogendra Singh Yadav?" Yogendra was still too sleepy to make any sense of the situation, "The name card over the bed says so. Please let me sleep. It is too late." She did not budge and insisted on knowing his name, army number and rank name. Yogendra realized it would be best to let her have the information, so that she would leave him alone. As soon as Yogendra gave the information, the nurse left in a hurry. Yogendra attempted to go back to sleep.

Within a few minutes, the MNS was back at his side. She instructed, "Give me the details of your family." Doubts began to fill Yogendra's mind immediately. Someone was here collecting information so late in the night. This did not give rise to a comfortable feeling within him. His mind began to think of the worst scenarios. It was obvious for Yogendra to think that something severe had happened at home for which they were in need of the information. Yogendra grew worried with every second. He had multiple questions in his head. Yogendra had seen on the news that there had been a blast on the Punjab mail. He knew that his brother had returned to duty after his holidays. Jitendra may have been assigned to that sector. Yogendra was stressed wondering if something had happened to his brother. Yogendra could not hold his inquisition anymore, "Madam, please tell me what is wrong?" The nurse did not budge, "First you tell me all the information." She noted the names of all the family members of Yogendra and their addresses. Despite Yogendra's efforts, she did not tell him anything and left the room after he shared the details.

Yogendra could not sleep for the rest of the night. His mind was too distressed to turn off. Yogendra's thoughts constantly went back to his family. He was awake when the nurse came back again at five in the morning. Yogendra had been waiting for the nurse to return and give him some information. The nurse noticed that Yogendra was awake, "Come on get up and get ready. The Chief is coming to meet you." Yogendra was surprised, "Me? Why would he want to meet me?" The nurse jerked her shoulder, "I do not have any idea. You should get ready. Shave your beard and freshen up." Yogendra was trying to process things, "Alright that is fine but how am I going to shave with a single hand? I need a barber's assistance." The nurse looked irritated, "Why can't you do it yourself?" Yogendra laughed, "Madam, you would know if you had ever shaved. It is not possible to shave with one hand." Yogendra's left hand was still going through recovery. He could not make sudden movements. The nurse did not argue, "Okay. A barber will be sent to you. When the ward master comes, ask him to give you news clothes and bed sheets. Clean yourself and prepare for the day."

After the nurse left, the barber and the ward master came in. The barber helped him shave and change his clothes. The warden changed the bed sheets for the entire room. They were all decked up and ready to meet the Chief. At around seven thirty in the morning there was hustle around the corridors which indicated that Chief V.P. Malik had arrived. The Command Head of the hospital escorted Chief into the room. Yogendra was sitting on his bed when the Command Head pointed towards him, "Sir, this is Yogendra Singh Yadav." Sharp black eyes looked towards him accompanied by a smile on the big round face. The tall, stout man approached his bed, "Congratulations soldier!" Yogendra was confused, "Thank you, Sir but why are you congratulating me?" Chief Malik laughed, "Don't you watch television?" Yogendra nodded, not being able to understand the reason behind the laughter. The Chief continued, "You must be watching movies then?" Yogendra did not want him to get the wrong impression so he quickly defended, "No, Sir. We do watch the news as well."

Chief Malik decided to test Yogendra's statement, "If you watch the news, tell me the most important news from yesterday." Yogendra was aware of current affairs. He had seen the news yesterday and rejoiced at the victory of his companion. Yogendra confidently answered, "There was an announcement yesterday that four soldiers were being awarded the Param Vir Chakra for their valour in the Kargil War. One among them was my companion in 18 Grenadiers." The Chief smiled, "Son, the award belongs to you." Yogendra had never been more surprised, "Mine? But I am alive. The news mentioned it was going to Singh who had expired on the field." V.P. Malik explained, "There was some error in administration. You both had the same names which created confusion. When we matched the army number with the dead bodies, it was found that there was no body matching that number. Signal was then sent out to all the base hospitals. Yesterday night, we found out you were here, so, I have come here to meet you. Now will you tell me what happened on your mission?"

Yogendra had forgotten all about the statement sent by the CO. He narrated the things that came from his heart. Every detail was narrated just as he had witnessed them. V.P. Malik sat on Yogendra's bed right opposite to him. He listened to every word attentively. Yogendra was in awe of this big personality sitting on his bed like a friend. Despite being such a powerful man, the Chief was grounded and down-to-earth. Yogendra was impressed by his behaviour and thought to himself if he ever reached such a position, he would want to be as kind as the Chief. Yogendra did not feel any hesitation while telling him the story. His voice shook as he recalled the details. This was the first time since recovery that had been recalling every second of the mission. The Chief felt the pain and longing in his voice. A nineteen year old boy had lost a lot and learnt humongous during the journey. After Yogendra completed his narration, the Chief patted him on his arm, "I am sorry son for the confusion. This is your award and you truly deserve it. Heartiest congratulations to you and your Platoon for earning this honour."

Yogendra was still in shock as he tried to soak in the wishes. The Chief enquired, "Does anyone come to meet you?" Yogendra replied, "Yes, Sir. My wife and people from my unit come to visit quite often." Chief Malik stood up from the bed, "Your wife? Where is she now?"

Mentioning Reena brought a smile on Yogendra's face, "The hospital gate has been closed today for your arrival, Sir. She must be waiting outside the gate." The Chief prepared to leave, "Alright next time when I come, I am going to meet your wife. If you need anything at all, reach out to me. I will surely try to help you." Yogendra stood up to salute the Chief, "Thank you so much, Sir. It means a lot to me that you came." With that Chief V.P. Malik left for the Independence Day ceremony at the Red Fort.But before going Chief handed his wrist watch to Yogendra as a token of appreciation from his side. After he left, the gates of the hospital were opened for visitors. As soon as Reena entered the room, people began to congratulate her. She had no clue what was happening. Reena looked expectantly at Yogendra for an explanation.

Yogendra informed, "Chief V.P. Malik has come to announce that I have been awarded the Param Vir Chakra." Reena kept staring at Yogendra, "And what is that?" Yogendra laughed out loud at Reena's simplicity. Most villagers did not have knowledge about these things. All members in Reena's family were civilians. They had no clue about army ranks or awards. He needed these people in his life who would keep him grounded. They did not care if he was a PVC awardee. For them he was still their Yogendra. He then explained, "Param Vir Chakra is the highest honor in the army. Have you read the story of Abdul Hamid?" Reena nodded in agreement. Yogendra continued, "Yes. This is the same medal as Abdul Hamid's story." Reena then gradually understood what Yogendra had achieved. People kept coming into his room to find Yogendra and congratulate him. Reena watched as Yogendra was circled by the soldiers asking him different questions. She wished the entire family could be here to watch this joyous moment.

More officers came to know about Yogendra's success and the visits continued. Chief V.P. Malik went back and informed the Colonel of 18 Grenadiers Regiment Balwan Singh, "I just came back from my meeting with your Param Vir Chakra hero." The Colonel was surprised, "Do you mean you went to heaven to meet him?" The

Chief laughed out, "So let me tell you a story of confusion." The chief then explained how the identities had been mixed for there were two Yogendras in the regiment. The Colonel had to see it for himself and verify the news. He went to meet Yogendra the very next day. The Colonel listened to all that Yogendra experienced in the last two day, "I could not believe this had happened. We are so sorry about the confusion and wrong information getting out and creating distress for your family." Yogendra was still trying to absorb the situation. He could not believe that such important people were apologizing to him. The apologies continued for a few days. The media houses also started crowding the hospital. Yogendra gave several interviews in a day but the CO's letter remained closed. He said everything from his heart and just as it had happened. The journalists also appreciated Yogendra's candour and simplicity.

A few days before the award ceremony, Major Kushal Thakur had come to visit Yogendra. His was the last face that Yogendra had remembered before his eyes closed on the battlefield. The man looked as kind as he had remembered. Yogendra was surprised that he could make time to visit him. Major Thakur greeted, "Congratulations to you, son. You have been very brave and made us all proud." He did make Yogendra feel like a son. His fatherly guidance had been effective throughout Yogendra's life. Major Kushal continued, "I am also here to tell you a few things that you need to remember. Son, this journey has turned you from a plant to a tree. This tree has a lot of fruit. When the fruits are ripe the branches of the tree droop down for the people to be able to get the fruits and eat them. However, the trees that have branches that remain stiff and straight are the ones whose fruits remain inaccessible. So, neither you become a tree whose branches are so stiff that the people find you arrogant nor the one whose branches touch the ground. Once the fruit touches the ground it catches insects and gets spoiled. This means that you should not be too timid and amicable for people to take advantage of your abilities. You have to create a balance in your life." Yogendra keeps the learning close to his heart. This has helped him become a better person in the future.

On 26th December, 2000, the day had finally arrived when Yogendra was going to be presented with the most prestigious award. He was still in the hospital recovering from his injuries. In the meantime, he had also received a promotion from his company. Yogendra had been given the rank of a Havaldar. The Government of India had invited him to receive the award from the President along with his family. Yogendra had been taken to the venue from the hospital. His parents and wife had come to cheer him on. The families of other winners were also present. Captain Vikram Batra's and Lieutenant Manoj Kumar's fathers had come to represent them while Rifleman Sanjay Kumar was supported by his family. Yogendra had never been to such an event and to add to it was visiting Rashtrapati Bhavan. The huge residence towered over him as Yogendra got down from the car. Yogendra was mesmerized by the beauty of the place.

Yogendra's parents and wife had already reached before him. They waited for him at the entrance. Yogendra and his family were guided by caretakers inside the premises. His eyes moved around the beautiful gardens. The area was majestic and people could easily get lost without a guide. Yogendra was delighted to experience this event with his family. Once they reached the conference hall, people were guided to allocated seats. The families were asked to sit in a certain section together while the soldiers and representatives accepting the award sat on one end. Yogendra sat beside a tall, fair middle aged man who later introduced himself as Giridhar Lal Batra, father of Vikram Batra. Yogendra struck a conversation with the soft spoken man, "Sir, I had the opportunity to meet Capt. Vikram on the field. He was a brave soldier and a humble man. We all are very proud of him." A parent is the happiest to hear praises for their children. Mr. Batra spoke with glistening eyes, "Yes, he has made us all proud. I have lost my son but the sacrifice he has made for the country has put us in this position to accept this award on behalf of him. We could have never imagined being part of such glory and excellence. However, his loss cannot be fulfilled by anything in the entire world."

Yogendra put right hand on Mr. Batra's shoulder consoling him. He understood his emotions. The middle-aged man got to see the glory but lost the son who was the reason behind this. The pain of parents losing their children cannot be measured. His eyes were red and shoulders had dropped as if pulling the weight of the world. Very few words struggled to come out of his mouth. During the majority of the event, his eyes seemed to be lost in the distance as if waiting for his son to appear out of nowhere. Yogendra knew no consolation could fill the vacuum, yet he continued, "The medal that your son has won is a symbol of the lives of all martyrs. The stories of all their sacrifices will forever be etched in this honour. Your love and teachings had given him the power to be selfless. He has created history for all of us and the entire nation shall remain grateful for his outstanding service." These words seemed to have calmed the man in that moment. When his son's name was announced, Mr. Batra could not hold back his tears anymore.

Yogendra had never been so excited in his life. Sitting in that hall, Yogendra felt electricity running through his body. His parents and wife were sitting in the audience. Whenever Yogendra looked up at them, they smiled and waved at him. He was not the only one charged by the spirit of the day. When Yogendra's name was announced to go up on the stage, he could not believe the moment. He walked up in front of the President. With his broken and bandaged arms, he accepted the award. The President congratulated him for his valour. Photographers all around them took pictures. Things kept happening in a trance like motion. When Yogendra walked down the stairs, he realized that his dream had come true. Things that he had only imagined in his dream had finally happened in reality. Yogendra touched the medal on his uniform trying to make himself believe that it was all real. People around him clapped in his honour. A village boy from Aurangabad could never have imagined this could actualize. Yogendra walked to his family who were a huge reason behind his success. He truly believed that the blessings of his parents and the nation had made it possible. It was also his wife's love that saved his life at the most crucial moment. The most important sacrifice for Yogendra was the one made by six of his companions. He believed that even after their blessings and sacrifice had cast a spell and created a shield around him that protected him in the most dangerous situations.

Yogendra watched his parents and wife waiting for him. His mother walked towards him and hugged him, "My son, you have made us so happy." She had tears in her eyes as she touched the medal on his coat. Yogendra's father also had tears in his eyes. He had never seen his father cry. Yogendra's father said, "Every father wants their son to be successful in life and fulfil all dreams. Today you have fulfilled my dream by becoming a great soldier. I have fought in the wars of 1965 and 1975 but never had been graced with such honour. You have made your place in the world and put us in a prestigious place in society. I can gladly say that today I will be known as the father of Yogendra Singh Yadav. I am proud of you, son." Yogendra's eyes turned moist and throat was dry. He had not expected such words from his father. His eyes shifted to Reena who did not say anything verbally but had a huge smile that made a statement. Yogendra's mother could not stop her tears. Yogendra consoled, "Maa, please don't cry. I am fine now." She smiled, "These are happy tears son. I am so relieved that you are safe and healthy. I am happier for your safety than the award. For me, you are more important than any award. If you were not here with us today, this award would not have given us any joy. You are my biggest award, son."

When Yogendra went back home after several months of recovery at the hospital, he had already become a hero. People in his village may not have learned enough to have any knowledge of the Param Vir Chakra but they did understand the essence of the award. Yogendra had been escorted by his brother. On his way, he met several people who recognized him and congratulated him. Some even asked him questions about his experience. Yogendra was surprised by these encounters and overwhelmed when they made him feel like a celebrity. When Yogendra reached home, he saw a crowd of people had gathered around his house. There were people playing drums and dancing to its rhythm. His family had joined the villagers in welcoming him. His mother had an 'aarti' platter to bless him. People came running with garlands and flowers. His cousin brother said, "You have held up the family name, brother. You have made your nation proud and I couldn't be happier for you." Within minutes his friends were pulling him into their celebration. They picked him up on their shoulder and went parading around the village. Held up on his companion's shoulder, Yogendra looked up at the sky imagining the lost ones smiling back at him."

Epilogue

10 Years Later

On 26th January, 2009, Yogendra landed back in the laps of the mountains that had once embraced him. On the occasion of Kargil Vijay Diwas, Yogendra visited Kargil as a chief guest of the ceremony. The program had been organized at the army base camp in Kargil. The entire venue has been decorated with huge tricolor flags. Yogendra's eyes traced the roads and the mountains. So much had changed around the place over the years. Yogendra could not believe that they had fought a war in these mountains. Yet every peak had a story to tell. It nourished the screams of the martyred soldiers. Every nook and corner reminded him of his days during the war. The routes they took to climb the mountain and the where they took guard from the attacks were clearly etched in his mind. Every object of nature in Kargil stands as a witness to the courage and sacrifice of the Indian soldiers. They had spent every last drop of their blood for their nation and every citizen is grateful for their service.

The event consisted of a parade by the soldiers and hoisting of the flag by the Home Minister of India. The guest had been facilitated with flowers and mementos. There were other musical performance. Around the end of the event, the chief guests had been requested to speak. Yogendra had been called to share his thoughts with the young soldiers. He had never been one of a public speaker. However, that day, he had been gripped by emotions. Yogendra address the crowd, "On the occasion of this special day, I wish every soldier and citizen of this country Happy Vijay Diwas. Although I am not entire sure the experience was a completely happy one. The outcome of the victory had bestowed all of us with abundant joy but the war had snatched away precious lives. I had lost friends and companions whose absence cannot be ever fulfilled. As a nineteen year old boy there were several things I had not processed. In the age, we often go with the flow of things. However, after winning the Param Vir Chakra, for several years, I had questioned my existence. Why did I survive when my companions perished? The question to that was answered a few years ago when Hanuman Thapa escaped an avalanche in the snow-capped mountains."

There was pin drop silence around the ground. Only the chirping of the birds accompanied Yogendra. Everyone was engrossed in the first-hand experience being shared by Yogendra. He continued, "About nine soldiers had been trapped under the ice and Hanuman had been rescued. He expired after a few days of treatment in the hospital. Then is when it struck me. Hanuman had survived to tell the story of his dead companions. I understood that every human is destined to die but it is what we do while living that matters. Our land that we call a mother truly embraces us in her arms. We give our lives for her and she like a mother protects our memories. A mother never lets the act of bravado and sacrifice made by her children get buried and unheard. She makes one of her children the medium to translate the story of their heroism to the world. Hanuman Thapa had lived to tell the story of their struggle in the mountains. In the same manner, I lived to tell the story of the struggle between the period of life and death that my fellow soldiers endured during the Kargil War."

Many of the soldiers in their eyes as they related to Yogendra's words. They would also be ready to give their lives for their nation or live to tell the tale. Yogendra concluded, "It is unimaginable the amount of emotional strength a soldier needs to possess to detach himself from the world. A boy from a village has to leave behind family, friends, and everything he loves for the most precious form of love for his country. The academy prepares a soldier for such a life where his companions become his only family. A soldier lives for his nation. Our responsibilities for the nation is primary and all other bonds are secondary to it. On the field the life of my companions become as precious as my own. Therefore, even after death the stories of many of my brave companions live within me and I deliver it to the world. This is the purpose of my life. Jai Hind!" Yogendra's speech was met with applause. It touched the heart of the soldiers and turned out to be a learning experience for all.

Yogendra, on the other hand, travelled on the road of nostalgia. Memories flashed before his eyes. On his way back, he kept recalling the moments and reliving the good ones in his mind. The narrow mountain roads were blocked by the convoys. Yogendra was looking out of the window starring at the ice capes lost in his thoughts. He was suddenly jolted back by a tapping on his window. A little boy of around eleven years was tapping his window with his right hand, while his left hand held a bunch of flowers. The boy had stunning eyes which immediately captured Yogendra. His milky white skin had become red from the cold outside. Yogendra rolled down the glass and a burst of cold wind entered the car. The boy requested in a childlike voice, "Please buy some flowers." Yogendra kept on looking without an answer. The boy pointed at the flowers, "Your missus will love them. They remain fresh for a week." Yogendra had never really bought flowers for Reena. It would be a good surprise, he thought. He pulled out a note from his pocket and held it out to the boy. As soon as the boy heard the cars ahead moving, he counted the change quickly and handed it back with the flowers.

Yogendra stared at the beautiful long-stemmed red flowers wrapped in a packet. Suddenly, a thought surfaced, he did not know the name. It would be quite embarrassing if his wife ended up asking as he had never seen such flowers in his hometown. The engine of the car had started and the boy had turned to walk away. Yogendra called out quickly, "Hey champ! What do you call these?" The blue eyes sparkled and a toothy smile appeared, "Tulips, Sir." Yogendra never forgot that name. Tulips. Ofcourse, he had to find them. Yogendra looked up at the sky from his window, "Do you have any more wishes my friend? I am at your service."